Healing Secondary Trauma

HEALING SECONDARY TRAUMA

Proven Strategies for Caregivers
and Professionals to Manage Stress,
Anxiety, and Compassion Fatigue

Trudy Gilbert-Eliot, PhD

ROCKRIDGE
PRESS

To the first responders and military personnel
I have treated: Your courage in overcoming
trauma was a privilege and an honor to witness.

CONTENTS

INTRODUCTION

No one would deny that a trauma survivor, someone who's lived through a frightening, life-threatening experience, might need help coping with the psychological aftermath. But we're only starting to recognize the impact that traumatic events have on people who experience them secondhand. Police officers, emergency room doctors and nurses, firefighters, military personnel, and other first responders all have to witness extreme violence as part of their jobs. Therapists, 911 operators, and health-care workers may find themselves inundated with upsetting imagery and descriptions of harrowing events . . . as can anyone who's helping a spouse, family member, or close friend recovering from trauma. If you fall into one of these categories, you may not realize that exposure to the traumatic experiences of others can take a significant toll on your own physical and mental health.

Secondary trauma is a real thing, and it can produce real symptoms. But too often, it's not discussed, even in professions where exposure to trauma is part of the job. There may be a workplace culture in a police department, hospital, or firehouse that assumes everyone will figure out for themselves how to cope with the effects of trauma. A memo or a staff meeting on the subject may elicit jokes or frivolous comments that lead everyone to keep their emotional experiences to themselves. A spouse or family member may have no resources or support to help them deal with the emotional burdens of caregiving.

Though a licensed psychotherapist, I myself had little understanding of secondary trauma until I experienced it. I was running errands one Friday when I received a call to come to an Air National Guard base in Reno, Nevada, following a plane crash. This was ten days after I'd assisted at the site of a mass shooting. After spending time with both sets of survivors, debriefing them and listening to their experiences with trauma, I couldn't close my eyes without seeing the stories I'd absorbed. I had trouble sleeping. I struggled with eating. As weeks passed, it took a conscious effort to control my emotions. I felt deep sadness; I felt raw and thin-skinned. I cried easily, which is not my nature, and I developed horrible insomnia and a lack of appetite.

I tried reaching out to some colleagues, but their unhelpful responses shut me down. They changed the subject after visibly becoming uncomfortable, offering no comforting words and not asking questions. I withdrew further into my own shell. It was weeks more before I sought out my own treatment and began the journey back to full functioning.

Over the next several months I began poring over the clinical literature to figure out what had happened to me, and I finally found a name for it: secondary trauma. I read everything about it that I could get my hands on. Soon I was teaching workshops to therapists, child welfare workers, nurses, and others about this phenomenon, which impacts so many who care for others in their work and private lives. I shared my own experiences and the tools that I'd used to take better care of myself. I spoke openly, sometimes making others uncomfortable, and healed myself even more.

If you are in one of the career fields mentioned previously, or if someone close to you is recovering from a traumatic experience, you most likely have also been exposed to trauma. Maybe you suspect that this has affected you but can't quite articulate how. *Healing Secondary Trauma* will help you understand the various ways that exposure to trauma can impact your thoughts, feelings, relationships, and physical health. And it will empower you with the best tools and techniques to heal, protect, and strengthen your own well-being as you continue to bring care and support to others in your profession and your life.

HOW TO USE THIS BOOK

We all respond differently to trauma. This is *your* journey, so consider this book a road map or guidebook, one to use according to your priorities, at your own pace. This may not necessarily mean reading it from front to back (though you certainly could do that if it suits your needs). After chapter 1's overview of secondary trauma and its effects, you may want to skip to the chapters that feel most relevant. If you struggle with anger, sadness, burnout, or other emotional issues, see chapter 2. In chapter 3, you'll learn how secondary trauma leads to negative thinking, self-blame, and other forms of dysfunctional thought. Chapter 4 explores the impact of secondary trauma on your physical health, and chapter 5 focuses on strengthening relationships with friends, family, partners . . . and yourself. And in chapter 6 you'll find advice for staying healthy and strong over the long term, particularly if you're in a career or living situation that will continue to expose you to secondary trauma. The symptoms of secondary trauma can change, so you might find yourself drawn to different chapters as your healing journey progresses.

Each chapter in *Healing Secondary Trauma* contains exercises based on the best clinical knowledge available, teaching you healthy strategies you can employ in your everyday life. Purchase a notebook or journal to accompany this book, and use it to complete the exercises (especially the "Go Deeper" exercises, which offer more in-depth techniques for reflection and self-assessment). Repeat the exercises whenever you need to, marking down the date each time so you can track your progress. Feel free to skip over exercises that seem too difficult, and circle back to them when you're ready. Also use your notebook to chronicle the thoughts, feelings, and reactions that arise along the way.

CHAPTER 1

Understanding Secondary Trauma

What is it that you want to change in your life? For someone who's been exposed to secondary trauma, that simple question can elicit a long list of answers. But most of them can be summed up by an equally simple statement: "I don't feel like myself anymore."

Perhaps friends have commented that you don't socialize the way you used to. Maybe family members are walking on eggshells to avoid triggering your temper, or your spouse has to sleep in a different bedroom because you wake up with nightmares. Maybe you feel anxious all the time, or you feel jumpy whenever you leave the house, or you bury yourself in self-criticism. You might have more aches and pains than you used to or feel constantly exhausted. Whatever your symptoms, however they affect you, your family, your friends, your job . . . you may wonder if you can ever feel like the person you used to be, before exposure to trauma affected you. This book answers that question with a resounding "yes." Of course the goal is not that you will feel exactly like you used to feel, but you will become appreciative of how you have grown, become stronger, and are much more resilient than before your trauma. You can discover new skills and a new sense of purpose in your life.

The journey to recovery isn't an easy one. But it begins here, and as with any journey, it's important to know where you're starting from. In this chapter we'll take an overview of secondary trauma, exploring what it is and who is at risk for it. We'll explore the effects that secondary trauma can have and focus on identifying and prioritizing the symptoms that are most problematic for you.

What Is Secondary Trauma?

Janice, a 911 operator, sits with her head bowed, struggling to describe her experiences. "I can't sleep," she says. "And when I do sleep, I have nightmares. Horrible nightmares about my work. They don't make sense!" she states, with obvious pain and frustration in her voice. "I never see the people I talk to, but they show up in my dreams, and it doesn't make sense!"

Teresa was visiting with a friend whose husband had been released from the hospital after a severe car accident. She became concerned when her friend grew agitated as the conversation circled around to the car crash. "I don't want to talk about it," she said angrily. "I'm sick of hearing him talk about it! It just makes me scared hearing it over and over." Teresa's friend remained uncharacteristically angry and agitated throughout their visit, and Teresa left earlier than she'd planned.

These are just two examples of what secondary trauma can look like. Sometimes called "vicarious trauma," it's a phenomenon that can impact anyone who's in a position to interact with a traumatized person: home health workers, police officers, firefighters, paramedics, therapists, nurses. Someone taking care of an ailing family member, like Teresa's friend, can also experience it.

Simply put, secondary trauma is indirect exposure to a traumatic event, usually by listening to a survivor's detailed narrative of the traumatic experience. Witnessing the event, or viewing photographs or videos of it, can also cause secondary trauma.

Like Janice, and Teresa's friend, people impacted by secondary trauma can seem emotionally changed or damaged; they can develop thoughts and behaviors that are out of character for them. Friends and family may feel that their whole personality is different. They can also develop physical symptoms, including difficulties sleeping and eating, cardiovascular problems, and other chronic health problems.

Trauma versus Secondary Trauma

Trauma can be defined as any event that overwhelms our normal coping resources and harms our mind or body. Typically, this event is life-threatening or threatens one's physical or psychological integrity. Examples include physical harm, emotional abuse, bullying, threats to one's community, sexual abuse, neglect, and exposure to danger in one's profession (like police officers, soldiers, or firefighters). We might call that "direct" trauma, though it's more commonly just termed *trauma*.

Secondary trauma happens when *someone else* is harmed physically or emotionally, but it has an effect on us. This trauma is secondhand because we didn't experience it ourselves as direct, personal trauma; it happened to someone else, and we're exposed by hearing the story and being emotionally impacted by it or simply by working with trauma survivors and witnessing the impact trauma has on them.

Sometimes people affected by secondary trauma don't realize the source of their distress. Consider a mother who listens to her daughter talk about repeatedly experiencing domestic violence at the hands of her ex-boyfriend. She feels her daughter's emotions almost as strongly as if she herself had been harmed. Soon she finds herself uncontrollably angry or sad at times and has other periods when she feels shut down or numb. Yet she doesn't connect all these symptoms to a common cause . . . after all, it's her daughter who was abused, not her.

Who's at Risk for Secondary Trauma?

Secondary trauma can impact anyone, but certain groups are at higher risk because of the work they do. If you're in any of these roles, you're more likely than the average person to experience secondary trauma:

Law enforcement workers. This group can include police officers, corrections officers, detectives, and crime scene analysts. On any given day, someone working in law enforcement might respond to a call to help a survivor of domestic violence, examine the scene of a violent homicide, take a report about a missing child, interview a rape survivor, or break up a fight between inmates in a jail. Investigators who take witness statements or interview crime victims may have multiple exposures to deeply disturbing details of traumatic crimes.

Firefighters. Firefighters are regularly exposed to the pain and suffering of others while responding to everything from traffic accidents to collapsed buildings to house fires. Long shifts and sleep deprivation amplify the emotional toll of interacting with people on the worst day of their lives. Like law enforcement officers, firefighters work closely with a group of coworkers, all of whom may be similarly impacted by trauma. This can lead to symptoms of secondary trauma being disregarded or dismissed as job stress.

Paramedics/emergency medical technicians. Paramedics, EMTs, and similar emergency medical workers are dispatched to help people who are injured for any number of reasons, including violent crime, accidents, falls, and burns. Contact with distressed family members can also take its toll.

Mental health therapists. Any mental health clinician who works with trauma survivors is at risk of secondary trauma. Patients in intense emotional pain will share their stories over and over again while the therapist asks searching questions, helping them understand that their reactions are normal. Because therapy happens in private and there are laws governing disclosure, many therapists don't have anyone else to talk to about their work. As a result, their struggles with secondary trauma may go unaddressed, affecting the therapist's ability to function at work and at home.

Emergency room staff. Doctors, nurses, and all ER personnel may have multiple exposures to trauma during every shift, not only from patients with life-threatening injuries but also from their highly emotional family members.

Child welfare workers. These professionals may respond to physical, sexual, emotional, or neglect abuse cases. Hearing trauma stories regarding children can be especially painful. Writing reports and conducting regular assessments of families repeat their exposure to trauma. They can also be impacted by having to remove children from their homes, which can cause additional trauma to the children.

Spouses and family members of people in trauma-prone professions. Partners, family members, and caregivers of active duty military personnel, veterans, first responders, law enforcement personnel, and firefighters are often studied in regard to secondary trauma. Not only do people in this category experience secondary trauma from the recounting of a loved one's combat experience or on-the-job dangers, but they're directly affected by any symptoms that the trauma produces in their family member.

Caregivers of someone with a serious medical issue. Some caregivers experience secondary trauma from their loved one's experiences with difficult medical interventions. The invasiveness of certain treatment protocols can be unavoidably traumatic to witness or experience. Furthermore, patients may regularly share descriptions of their emotional and physical pain, which may be very disturbing for the caretaker.

Valeria's Story

Valeria had been a firefighter for twelve years. She felt very proud to be one of only four women to make it through the very rigorous fire academy in her county and quickly became integrated into the firefighter culture of hard work, bravery, and a stoic approach to hardship. But things changed when she responded to a house fire where she helped suppress the flames while others attempted to rescue two people trapped inside.

Over the next several days, Valeria played the scene over and over in her mind, especially the screams and crying of the family whose loved ones were trapped in the house. As weeks turned into months, she became more irritable, found little pleasure in her work or her time off, and struggled to get enough sleep. She avoided conversations with other firefighters, which used to be a favorite part of her workday. And she felt much more negative about herself and others.

Finally, John, a fellow firefighter, approached her. John was highly respected for his bravery and was frequently held up as an example of an ideal firefighter. He pointed out that he'd noticed the change in Valeria, then shared a similar experience of his own. John described how at first he thought he could handle the lack of sleep and anger, until his wife helped him see that he couldn't overcome it by himself. He went on to explain this wasn't the stress of the job that was affecting Valeria; it was trauma.

John pointed Valeria in the direction of some resources for support. She saw a therapist, who conducted a thorough assessment and helped Valeria understand and process her trauma reactions. She learned relaxation techniques that allowed her to manage her anxiety. Valeria's mood improved, and she once again looked forward to going to work every day.

That's not an exhaustive list; other groups impacted regularly by trauma include funeral directors, coroner's office staff, attorneys representing victims of hate crimes, and staff who work at a rape crisis center. The common thread is exposure to someone else's trauma through one's work or personal life. If that applies to you, then secondary trauma is a concern, even if your specific situation isn't listed on pages 4–5.

Understanding Your Range of Symptoms

Valeria was fortunate to have a peer who recognized what she was experiencing; sometimes two people with secondary trauma have very few symptoms in common. And people who are continually being exposed to new trauma, such as police officers and paramedics, can develop symptoms that change over time as they process new experiences. Some symptoms impact our mental health, while others manifest as physical issues, including high blood pressure, gastrointestinal problems, and fatigue.

Let's begin your journey to recovery by zeroing in on the symptoms that are affecting your life.

Anxiety

Anxiety is a state of nervousness or worry. Sometimes anxiety feels like it has a clear cause: "I feel anxious when I have to give a presentation in front of my peers." Feeling anxiety about performing an activity that's difficult or new to us is normal. But sometimes anxiety seems free-floating, without a specific basis attached to it. Most of us have anxiety from time to time—it's part of life—but anxiety becomes a problem when it causes a great deal of distress and makes it very difficult for you to complete your obligations socially, at work, or in other areas of your life.

Exercise: Anxiety Self-Assessment

Answer the questions in this self-assessment, and the ones that follow, in your notebook. For each checklist, consider your behavior over the previous several months. Add any thoughts or descriptions related to the questioned behavior that come to you as you're working through the checklist. Include as much detail as you wish.

- Do I feel anxious when I am in a social situation where I must interact with people I don't know?

- Do I feel anxious when I must eat or drink with others around me?

- Do I feel anxious when I have to perform tasks with people watching, such as giving a presentation at work?

- Do I have fears that other people will notice I'm anxious?

- Do I try to find excuses to avoid social situations?

- Does worrying occupy a great deal of my thinking time?

- Do I find it difficult to control my worrying?

- When I worry, do I feel restless or on edge and/or have trouble sleeping?

- When I worry, do I become tired and/or have difficulty concentrating?

- When I worry, do I get irritable and/or have more muscle tension than usual?

- Does my anxiety or worry cause problems for me at work, at home, or with friends?

If you answer *yes* to more than two of these questions, spend some time thinking about the symptoms or behaviors related to your anxiety. Over the course of the next week, whenever you experience anxiety, write about it in your notebook. Make a list of situations likely to increase your anxiety, and refer to it as you learn symptom management techniques in the following chapters of this book.

Depression

Depression, like anxiety, is a state we all find ourselves in from time to time. But clinical depression is much more serious. Along with generally feeling down or unhappy, and experiencing little pleasure in your regular activities, signs of clinical depression include appetite disturbances, struggling with too little or too much sleep, feelings of worthlessness or excessive guilt, suicidal thoughts, low energy or fatigue, difficulty concentrating or making decisions, and feeling agitated or slowed down. When these symptoms last for over two weeks and cause a significant disruption in your ability to live your life, clinical depression is likely.

Exercise: Depression Self-Assessment
Answer the following questions in your notebook.

- Have I felt sad, down, or depressed almost every day for the last two weeks?

- Have my favorite activities, like hobbies or outings with friends or family, failed to give me the pleasure they usually do?

- Have I noticed myself eating much less, or much more, over the last few weeks?

- Have I noticed I've been sleeping very poorly or for many more hours than usual?

- Do I have a lot of guilt or hopelessness about my life?

- Have I had suicidal thoughts or considered self-harm?

- Have family and/or friends mentioned to me that they don't think I'm functioning as well as usual?

If you answer *yes* to more than five of these questions, spend time thinking about the symptoms you've experienced and how they affect your behavior. Has depression prevented you from functioning at work or at home? If so, see your doctor or a clinical therapist for a more detailed assessment.

Panic Attacks

A panic attack seems to come out of the blue, during an otherwise calm moment. Suddenly your heart rate accelerates and breathing becomes difficult. You might feel pressure on your chest; you might begin to sweat or shake. Dizziness, and numbness in your arms, hands, or feet, are often part of a panic attack. The incident usually lasts only 10 minutes or so, but during that time you may feel like you're dying. It's a frightening experience, and the fear of having another attack can affect the decisions you make, preventing you from socializing or doing the things you want to do.

Exercise: Panic Attack Self-Assessment

Answer these questions in your notebook. (The questions don't apply to times when you were exercising or exerting yourself.)

- Have you experienced a time when you escalated from a calm state to a state of panic?

- Have you experienced your heart rate accelerating out of the blue, when you are not exerting yourself?

- Have you experienced difficulty breathing, when not exercising, that appears randomly?

- Have you felt like you have pressure on your chest that comes on suddenly and doesn't make sense based on what you are doing?

- Have you started to sweat or shake while performing normal activities or when doing nothing?

- Have you had times when you have felt your arms, hands, or feet go numb suddenly, then return to full sensation a while later?

- When feeling any of these symptoms, have you also felt dizzy?

- When feeling any of these symptoms, have you ever had thoughts that you were dying?

If you answer *yes* to any of these questions, you may have experienced one or more panic attacks. Think about your symptoms and try to track them. How long do they usually last? How often do you experience them? Consult with your doctor as you explore ways to ease your anxiety with the techniques in this book.

Physical Symptoms

As we've noted, people exposed to trauma may develop physical problems along with the emotional and behavioral struggles. Trauma survivors may notice more gastrointestinal problems, asthma, heart palpitations, headaches, gynecological issues, chronic pain, and a compromised immune system. According to a study of over 38,000 people, trauma survivors with one qualifying traumatic life event were more likely to develop seven chronic illnesses, while those with five or more traumas were more likely to develop nine out of eleven illnesses investigated in the study (Scott et al., 2013).

Exercise: Physical Symptoms Self-Assessment

Consider your health over the past six months. Copy this list into your notebook and check off any symptoms you've experienced. Note how frequent and severe the experience was and any thoughts, descriptions of your behavior, or other details you choose.

- Stomach upset or digestion issues

- Frequent or severe headaches

- Asthma

- Racing heart rate

- Aches and pains

- Colds and/or flus every season

- Arthritis

- Back and neck pain

- High blood pressure

- Diabetes

- Peptic ulcer

- Heart disease

If you have any of these physical issues, focus more closely on them and try to determine when you first noticed them and how frequently you experience them. Return to this list as you learn to manage your secondary trauma symptoms, and note changes in the frequency and severity of your physical symptoms. If you have several physical symptoms on this list, consider bringing your workbook to your doctor, and discuss your trauma exposure. Your physician can help you address the physical symptoms while you work on the psychological symptoms.

Relationship Issues

If secondary trauma is affecting your life, it's probably affecting the people around you as well. Sometimes regular exposure to trauma on the job—and the need to always "be there" for others—causes emotional exhaustion, leaving you little compassion or empathy to offer the people close to you. This emotional distance or numbness can seem like rejection to a spouse or partner. Family and friends may need to deal with their loved one's irritability and anger, feeling like they have to walk on eggshells. A spouse may need to sleep in a separate bed due their partner's nightmares. After recovery from secondary trauma, couples or families might consider seeing a therapist to address any unhealthy habits and adaptations they fell into as a way of dealing with the trauma.

Exercise: Interpersonal Relationships Self-Assessment

If you suspect that trauma has affected your relationship with someone close, look back to a time in your life when you were feeling very well, when you were happy and operating at your best. Answer the following questions in comparison to that peak time in your life. Include any thoughts, descriptions of your behavior, and other details that seem relevant.

Compared to before I was exposed to trauma, do I:

- Have more memories that are unpleasant to recall?

- Avoid doing some activities?

- Experience a more restricted range of emotions?

- Take less pleasure in activities I used to enjoy?

- Feel less connected to the people in my life?

- Have negative thoughts more frequently?

- Sleep less well or deeply?

- Have more irritable or grumpy days?

Make a list of the relationships you believe have been most impacted by the behavior changes you identified in the list. Consider reviewing the checklist with those people. Allow yourself to listen to how your behavior appears to them. Commit to improving one or two of those behaviors as you start your recovery journey.

If You Need More Help

You might prefer to work through your difficulty on your own, but sometimes it's necessary to get professional help. If you are feeling suicidal, call the National Suicide Prevention Lifeline at (800) 273-8255 for 24/7 support. If you're having severe symptoms of any kind, including nightmares, flashbacks, depression, anxiety, or relationship distress, it's important to seek out a professional to obtain an assessment and treatment recommendations.

Your health insurance company likely has a list of clinical therapists in your area who specialize in needed areas such as trauma, depression, anxiety, and couples therapy. Some workplaces offer employee assistance programs that will provide a referral to a therapist and may assist with making the appointment. Or ask your primary care physician for a referral. There are many low-cost or no-cost clinics in larger cities, for those with no insurance coverage, and most universities offer therapy to local residents provided by therapists in training.

How Is Secondary Trauma Affecting You?

Some of the assessments you just completed may shine a spotlight on symptoms you hadn't connected with your exposure to trauma. Recovering from trauma exposure requires noticing not only the symptoms but the behaviors that you acquired to cope with them. For example, you might adjust to anxiety by not going out as often. You might manage irritability by spending more time away from people. You might avoid having difficult conversations with your spouse to prevent arguments that might trigger your anger. We'll conclude this chapter by prioritizing which symptoms are affecting you and identifying the behavior changes that come with them. Once you have a better understanding of how trauma has changed you, you can begin to build skills that will allow you to heal. We can group the symptoms of secondary trauma into these categories:

Intrusion Symptoms. Imagine you're standing at your sink washing dishes when you accidently drop a glass. It hits the bottom of the sink with a loud crash, shattering into small pieces. Suddenly you're flooded with memories of a fire you responded to, where windows were blown out from the heat of the fire, broken glass flew everywhere, and several victims were cut and injured as they fled from their house. You feel upset for hours after dropping the glass.

This is an example of an intrusion symptom. This category includes upsetting memories of the original traumatic incident, dreams that include content or emotions from the event, flashbacks, troubling feelings triggered by reminders of the incident, or strong physical reactions to reminders of the trauma (such as elevated heart rate).

Avoidance Symptoms. This group of symptoms includes any and all attempts to evade memories, thoughts, and feelings related to the trauma, along with avoiding people, places, activities, and objects that might be reminders of the traumatic experience. Avoidance is a strategy for preventing unpleasant emotions, but it often leaves us in a smaller and smaller world, making it progressively more difficult for us to live a full and fulfilling life.

Negative Changes in Thinking and Mood. As time goes by after a trauma, survivors try to find ways to explain the event to themselves. Sometimes this explanation slowly evolves into a healthy, accurate narrative that helps us understand what happened. But other times, the story we tell ourselves becomes progressively distorted and negative. We might leave out important details; develop deeply negative beliefs about ourselves, the world, or others; unfairly blame ourselves or others for causing the trauma; or harbor lingering strong feelings like horror, anger, and shame. These changes drain our interest in doing things that used to be pleasurable, distance us from the people around us, and make it difficult to feel positive emotions like love and happiness.

Altered Arousal. This is a symptom group that people most readily equate with trauma exposure. Sleep disturbance is a common symptom in the immediate aftermath of trauma, although it can linger and become an enduring problem. Other arousal symptoms include having trouble concentrating, startling easily, feeling needlessly watchful (a state called hypervigilance), taking undue risks, and being irritable or aggressive toward others.

Think through each of these symptom groups. Look back to a time in your life when you were doing very well. Consider how often you experienced each type of symptom then, compared to after your trauma. Ask a few people you are close to for honest feedback about any changes they've noticed. In your notebook, make a list of the symptoms that most apply to you, and use the list to guide your exploration through the rest of this book.

Exercise: Identify Priorities for Symptom Reduction

In your notebook, rate the severity of the following secondary trauma symptoms from 0 (not a problem) to 10 (extremely difficult problem). Base the rating on your experience with each symptom over the last month.

- Distressing memories of trauma

- Distressing dreams related to trauma

- Flashbacks

- Continuous negative emotional state like anger or anxiety

- Not regularly feeling positive emotions

- Having negative beliefs about yourself, the world, or others

- Avoiding doing activities you used to enjoy

- Regulating your emotions after being triggered

- The ease in which you go out in public

- Talking with others about your experiences with trauma

- Being interested in doing significant activities, like work, socializing, or hobbies

- Feeling connected or close to others

- Getting a restful night's sleep

- Struggling with concentration

- Startling easily

- Having anger outbursts

- Feeling hypervigilant

Review which symptoms have the highest ratings, and focus on those as you work your way through the rest of this book.

Return to the self-assessments in this chapter as you put the strategies in the rest of this book into practice. Repeat them and compare the results to see any changes taking place as you work on your recovery.

Exercise: Identify Priorities for Behavior Change

Rate each of the following behaviors "not true," "somewhat true," or "completely true," based on your experience over the past month. Write your answers in your notebook. Jot down any other thoughts that come up about the statements.

- Although I know it was difficult at the time it happened, when I think about my trauma now, I do not feel deeply disturbed.

- I rarely have bad dreams.

- I don't have flashbacks.

- I am not an angry or anxious person.

- I feel a full range of emotions that make sense in their intensity.

- For the most part I feel positive about myself, the people in my life, and the world around me.

- I thoroughly enjoy the activities I participate in.

- When something upsetting happens, I am able to regulate my emotions quickly and I don't allow it to affect the rest of my day.

- I am very comfortable in crowds and in public places.

- I feel comfortable talking about my experiences with trauma with safe people or professionals.

- I get interested and excited about participating in my normal activities.

- I feel very close and connected to significant people in my life.

- I can easily get a restful night's sleep.

- Concentrating hard on interesting activities is easy for me.

- I do not anger easily and very rarely act angry or irritable.

Look at your "not true" answers in this quiz. Determine which of these would enhance your life the most should they become "completely true." Highlight these in your notebook and focus on them as you move forward.

Takeaways:

+ Trauma is any event that overwhelms our normal coping resources and harms our mind or our body.

+ Secondary trauma is caused by an individual's exposure to the trauma of others, usually by hearing the story.

+ There are many types of professions and caregivers who are at risk of secondary trauma, including anyone who helps a family member recover from a traumatic event.

+ Being exposed to trauma can affect us in many ways, impacting our emotional and physical health and creating difficulties in our relationships.

+ Trauma can cause four different types of symptoms: intrusion symptoms, avoidance symptoms, negative thinking and mood, and altered arousal.

+ Trauma is very treatable; someone exposed to trauma can recover to become stronger and more engaged in life.

CHAPTER 2

Your Emotions

A sudden fit of rage over a minor event. A sadness so deep you don't want to leave the house. The emotional consequences of exposure to secondary trauma can be some of the most distressing symptoms—and the most confusing. When we find ourselves in the grip of a rage or debilitating sadness, we may not realize its connection to the trauma we've been exposed to—especially if it happens weeks or months later. You may wonder if you're losing your mind. But anxiety, sadness, fear, anger, a sense of helplessness, and many other emotions are common for those who are dealing with trauma. Some people find themselves in the grip of these strong emotions, acting out and behaving in ways not typical for them. Others react by doing everything they can to avoid having feelings, only to have them come out sideways at inopportune times.

The root of these symptoms is your brain's attempt to keep you safe. Anger, fear, and other emotional states prepare your body to respond to danger, the "fight-or-flight" reaction. But a brain that's overwhelmed with trauma—including secondary trauma—can have trouble turning off that reaction. Even when the trauma is past, the brain continues working in overdrive to figure out who, what, and where is safe or unsafe. You feel anxious, or irritable, or overwhelmed as this ongoing vigilance takes its toll on your emotions and energy level. All sorts of details—sights, sounds, smells related to the traumatic event—become interpreted as triggers, signals that there's danger. They spur your emotionally activated brain to push you toward anger, or panic, even though you're not consciously aware of what set off the alarm.

In this chapter, we'll take a closer look at the most common emotional symptoms associated with secondary trauma: anger, sadness, exhaustion (not just physical tiredness but feeling emotionally overwhelmed), and compassion fatigue—the erosion of the empathy that makes you an effective first responder, therapist, healer, or caretaker. You'll learn some ways that you can manage these and other emotional states. And we'll discuss some tactics for practicing and tracking the positive changes you want to make in your life.

Anger and Irritability

We all get angry. But anger we feel in our everyday lives usually has an identifiable cause—someone cut us off in traffic; our friend is late for an appointment *again*; our child didn't put away her toys. The anger that's a consequence of trauma, though, is not always easy to trace to its source.

Let's say your work as a paramedic has put you in contact with hundreds of accident victims and their family members, who all share the details and emotional stories of their incidents. After several years of this, you begin having heated outbursts at work. You become irritable and show visible anger to patients who could have, in your opinion, transported themselves instead of calling an ambulance and wasting your time. But those patients aren't really the problem. It's the secondary trauma, all the upsetting details and raw emotion from all those accident victims, that has you predisposed to react angrily. Your brain is stuck in threat mode, leaving you prone to anger as a way of readying yourself for the next danger. But all this happens behind the scenes. All you know is you have a short fuse, and certain patients are trying your patience.

We tend to think of anger as "bad," but anger itself is simply an emotional experience. It's the way we *express* our anger, the way we respond to it, that can be healthy or unhealthy. For example, consider the organization Mothers Against Drunk Driving (MADD), founded in 1980 to reduce fatalities and injuries caused by alcohol-impaired driving. It might be argued that the group was born partly from the anger of women affected by drunk-driving incidents.

Of course, we don't always respond to our anger in constructive ways. Often we lash out, loudly and ineffectively. Sometimes we try to ignore our anger and hope the feeling will go away. Broadly speaking, there are four basic ways we can address any emotion. Let's consider each, using anger as an example.

Escalate It. Whether flying into a rage or drafting a harshly worded e-mail, we tend to amplify our anger when we feel someone else is to blame for the situation. Or when we have a convenient target, like a spouse, a family member, coworkers, or even a stranger. If your brain has been primed by trauma, a minor event might seem like a severe threat or a sign of someone's malevolent intent, causing what might have been a brief moment of annoyance to surge into a fuming tantrum.

Avoid It. When our feelings are uncomfortable or fall into a "bad" category like anger, it's tempting to avoid or suppress them. We walk away from the problem and refuse to discuss it, or we change the subject or deny it even happened. This approach may seem to solve the problem, but consistently avoiding your anger doesn't work in the long run. Avoiding an emotion is like not cleaning out your house because you don't want to admit it's a mess: The more you refuse to address the problem, the more cluttered your psyche becomes. (Note that avoiding your anger isn't the same as *delaying* action on it. Sometimes it's healthier to put our feelings aside temporarily, until we're in an appropriate place to sort them out.)

Convert It. Sometimes we deal with a difficult emotion by converting it into something we find more acceptable. For example, secondary trauma could elicit feelings of helplessness in a father whose child was injured in a car accident. But to him, helplessness is a sign of weakness. So without being aware of it, he converts that uncomfortable helplessness to a less objectionable emotion, like anger. This leaves the primary emotion—helplessness—unaddressed, and therefore likely to keep coming back. Meanwhile, he continues to act on the secondary emotion, lashing out angrily with the slightest provocation, without understanding its true cause.

Manage It. The only truly healthy method for coping with your feelings is to *manage* the emotion. This means determining what emotions you're feeling and using healthy strategies to deal with them. A person who feels hurt or sad might seek comfort from others. Someone who's confused or overwhelmed could decide to ask for advice from someone who's been in a similar situation. When we feel hopeless, we might ask friends to remind us about areas where we are competent and capable. Healthy tactics for managing anger include assertiveness, problem solving, cognitive restructuring, and acceptance.

Exercise: What Are Your Triggers?

If secondary trauma is affecting you, it may sometimes feel like an outburst of anger or some other strong emotion comes out of nowhere. But these swells of emotion are almost always brought on by a trigger—a sight, sound, smell, or some other stimulus that your brain associates with the trauma you were exposed to. They fall into two categories: sensory triggers and feeling triggers.

Knowing the triggers for your anger or other emotions will help you manage the emotional symptoms of secondary trauma exposure. Read through the following roster of potential triggers, and in your notebook, create a list of any that were present when you had episodes of anger, adding any others that you've noticed. Watch for triggers going forward, and add them to your list. (It can be harder to identify feeling triggers, so see Go Deeper, page 30.) When you've identified your triggers, take steps to anticipate and prepare yourself to cope with them when you can, and to manage your anger with the techniques discussed in this chapter.

Sensory Triggers

- Sounds related to your trauma

  - Examples: yelling or screaming, gunfire, sirens, loud noises

- Smells related to your trauma

  - Examples: blood, dirt, vomit, gunpowder

- Visuals related to your trauma

  - Examples: places related to trauma, people related to trauma, memories of trauma, items related to trauma

- Tastes related to your trauma

  o Examples: blood, vomit, food eaten right before trauma occurred

- Physical sensations related to your trauma

  o Examples: temperatures or the weather; feeling skin, clothing, metal; pain, discomfort, muscle tension; weight as when carrying someone or something; racing heart rate

Feeling Triggers

- Rage, anger

- Fear, anxiety

- Hopelessness, powerlessness, sadness

- Any other feelings related specifically to your trauma

- Feelings that became connected to the trauma aftermath

  o Betrayal

  o Disappointment

  o Vulnerability

  o Confusion

- Anniversaries

Exercise: Releasing Anger

When you were young, did your parents ever send you to your room when you were throwing a tantrum or fighting with a sibling? It worked, didn't it? Calling a time-out is an incredibly effective strategy for managing anger, and you can use it yourself to make sure you don't act in ways that you might regret. The process is simple: When you feel yourself getting heated during an interaction with someone, announce that you need to step away and calm yourself down. If it's someone you know well, you can be honest. In other circumstances, give a simple excuse: "I want to finish this conversation, but I need to [use the restroom, attend a meeting, finish a project that is due]. So I'll touch base with you [pick a specific time at least a half hour later]."

It's best to take at least thirty minutes to cool off; it takes about that long for the physiology of anger to wear off as your body releases more calming chemicals into your bloodstream. During that time, it's useful to engage in some physical activity if you can: Go for a brisk walk or a run, play with a pet, work out, or even do some deep breathing exercises (see chapters 3 and 4). The activity will help release anger's grip on your body.

GO DEEPER:
Understanding Your Feeling Triggers

After you've identified some of your triggers on the list beginning on page 27, this worksheet can give you a better understanding of the feeling triggers that are affecting you. Copy the chart into your notebook, and fill it out when you experience a trigger that you can't identify. Repeat until you start to see patterns emerging. For example, if you were evaluating anger, you might notice you feel the most anger on Mondays and Tuesdays. The next step would be to consider what's different about Mondays and Tuesdays. Is your job more stressful on those days? Do you interact with different people? Take note of how you responded to your anger, and write down ways that you might manage it next time.

Date:_____

Day of the Week:_____

Intensity 1–10: Circle one: (low) 1 2 3 4 5 6 7 8 9 10 (high)

Estimate the duration/time of the feeling:_____

Story of the event:_____

People involved:_____

Body signs:_____

Thoughts:_____

How the feeling was used:
    ❑ Escalated It   ❑ Avoided It   ❑ Converted It   ❑ Managed It

How this was accomplished:_____

Any aggression:_____

Time-out used? Yes/No How Long?_____

Drug/alcohol use or cravings? Yes/No What did you do?

Rate Yourself:
(Handled Poorly) 1 2 3 4 5 6 7 8 9 10 (Handled Great)

Sadness and Hopelessness

We feel sad when a friend moves away, when our favorite supervisor takes a job elsewhere, or when someone we love dies. Sadness and hopelessness are natural responses to loss. Feeling sadness in relation to a secondary trauma event is also normal, as we adjust to the reality of the traumatic event. For example, a woman whose sister experienced a rape may feel that the world is not as safe as she thought it was. She might feel that she wasn't a good sister because she wasn't there to protect her sibling. It's the loss of that safety, and of her sense of self, that can cause her to feel sad and hopeless.

Sadness may come to you when you consider yourself capable of witnessing traumatic experiences on the job but find you can't handle it as well as you used to. You may feel sad when friends or coworkers don't notice your struggle or ask how you're doing. Feelings of hopelessness can arise if you're trying to manage your secondary trauma symptoms but aren't successful. Both sadness and hopelessness undermine our motivation to try new approaches, making it harder to find a solution.

When sadness and hopelessness linger, they leave us vulnerable to depression. As touched on in chapter 1, clinical depression is more than just ordinary melancholy. It's a long-lasting psychological disorder that can feel like a mix of sadness, hopelessness, and overwhelming powerlessness. Someone who's clinically depressed may spend days on end in bed, withdraw socially, stop doing activities that used to be fun, and feel a very limited range of emotions. People with depression regularly report anhedonia, which is defined as a state wherein the person feels little pleasure in activities, interactions, tasks, or life in general. Other symptoms include weight or appetite changes, problems with sleep, feeling little energy, thoughts of suicide, and feelings like excessive guilt or worthlessness. Sometimes a person who's experiencing depression doesn't recognize the severity of their disorder until a friend or loved one raises the issue.

Exercise: When Your Sadness Feels Too Deep

Emotions help us become motivated and organized to take important actions: If we feel afraid, we remove ourselves from danger. If someone makes us happy, we spend more time with them. And if we're sad, we might avoid the circumstances that made us feel that way. But sadness that's a consequence of secondary trauma can motivate us to act in ways that *perpetuate* the sadness: thinking and talking about sad experiences, avoiding doing anything pleasurable, isolating, staying in bed all day, moping, not interacting socially, crying all the time.

A strategy for managing this, which comes from dialectical behavior therapy (DBT), is to take the "opposite to emotion action"—that is, determine what your sadness is motivating you to do, and try to enact the opposite behavior. Here are some examples:

If your tendency is to be inactive, get moving. Go take a walk. Allow yourself to be in bed only during sleeping hours. Limit television or internet time to one hour a day.

If you're prone to avoiding other people, say yes to a social invitation at least once a week. Make yourself eat lunch in the staff break room around coworkers. Commit to talking to a friend every day. Clean your living space so you'll feel comfortable inviting someone over.

If you've stopped doing anything pleasant, reintroduce yourself to old pleasures. Restart an old hobby or sport you used to play. Have friends over for a potluck with your favorite foods. Reread a favorite book. Take a new exercise or dance class. Plan a trip.

A general antidote for sadness is to do things you have always been very good at, which will bring on feelings of hope and joy. If you're not sure where to start, check in with people who know you well to discuss the hobbies, tasks, chores, and goals that you've been successful with in the past.

Exhaustion and Burnout

We all know what it's like to be tired. And most of us have felt the kind of bone-tiring fatigue that we call exhaustion. But exhaustion that's associated with trauma can be physical or psychological. Physical exhaustion is typically caused by lack of sleep—we'll discuss in chapter 4 how trauma can disrupt sleeping patterns—or from overworking the body, or both. Psychological exhaustion is generally caused by an excess of stress, which makes us feel overburdened, ineffective, and, well, exhausted. When physical and psychological exhaustion occur together, we call it *burnout*. It's a state of being that leads to poor coping, low motivation, a negative view of self, and low self-esteem.

We most frequently see burnout as a response to job conditions. A number of workplace conditions make burnout more likely, including long hours, an overwhelming workload, pay that's not commensurate to the job, poor supervision, task ambiguity (i.e., job responsibilities are not well defined), lack of professional satisfaction on the part of the worker, and interaction with people who have chronic mental illness.

Burnout is much more common in public sector jobs as opposed to private company jobs. So law enforcement officers, firefighters, fire paramedics, nurses, child welfare workers, and many others who encounter secondary trauma on the job are more likely to develop burnout (Sprang, Craig, and Clark, 2011).

Unfortunately, both exhaustion and burnout make people more vulnerable to secondary trauma, and they make trauma symptoms harder to handle. Exhaustion drains your emotional bandwidth, making it difficult to access your coping skills. And burnout tends to bring an intense desire to escape, often leading people to seek distractions like watching television or playing video games. That means neglecting relationships, family responsibilities, personal care, and other areas of life that suffer when secondary trauma takes hold.

Exercise: Acceptance of Negative Emotions

Whether you're coping with anger, sadness, burnout, or other emotional effects of secondary trauma exposure, you probably feel locked in a battle, an ongoing struggle with your own emotions. One method of escaping this conflict follows the principles of acceptance and commitment therapy, or ACT. In this type of therapy, which is used to treat trauma and many other disorders, the primary goal is not to reduce your symptoms. Instead, this approach encourages a deeper acceptance of your feelings. When you recognize and accept the fact that you're feeling burned out, angry, or sad, instead of being upset by it and struggling against the feeling, you free up mental energy that you can use to manage the emotion more effectively. If you're feeling sad, you'll find it easier to reach out to someone for comfort. If you're feeling burned out, you'll find it easier to plan some downtime or make plans for a career change.

To try an ACT exercise, imagine yourself in the last emotionally difficult situation you experienced as a result of your trauma. Notice all the cues around you—the people, the location, the temperature, the sounds, the smells. Become aware of how all this makes you feel. What is the name of the feeling? Is it anger, sadness, anxiety, exhaustion? Where do you hold it in your body? If you had to describe this emotion, what would it look like? What is its color, size, and shape? Does it move or change? Does it have weight or have a temperature? As you get to know the feeling, just let it be; continue to notice it and any changes it goes through. Breathe and notice. How do you feel now? Has anything changed for you as you stop struggling with the feeling? Continue to make room for the emotion, allowing it to dissipate without trying to force it away. The more you do this following or even during an emotion, the easier you'll find it to accept your emotions and decide on the best ways to handle them.

Compassion Fatigue

Our brains are hardwired for empathy and compassion. It's one of the reasons that someone else's trauma can have such an impact on us. But like any physical or psychological capability, when we overuse our capacity to be compassionate, that ability becomes exhausted. Imagine starting your day listening to your daughter's emotional venting about how hard school is, then spending two hours at work as mediator for your staff who are having severe differences of opinion, then on your drive home talking with a friend who shares an update regarding her messy divorce . . . by day's end you find yourself having difficulty summoning empathy for your spouse, who wants to vent about his own difficulties. It doesn't mean you've stopped caring. But like leg muscles that become tired and shaky after a workout at the gym, the neural circuits in our brain that enable us to be compassionate also need rest when they're taxed.

Symptoms of compassion fatigue go beyond lapses in empathy: apathy, poor concentration, perfectionism, rigidity, negativity, irritability, and lowered self-esteem can all be part of the phenomenon. Compassion fatigue can make you feel less effective at your work, especially if your occupation requires you to be empathetic. Many of the trauma-prone jobs we're discussing in this book are inclined to cause compassion fatigue. After all, therapists, caretakers, police officers, and others who must be compassionate in their profession are at greater risk for overtaxing that ability.

Exercise: Regenerating Empathy

Fortunately, there are steps you can take when you're feeling like your compassion stores are running low. The next time you're feeling compassion fatigue, review this checklist. Write down the most relevant strategies in your notebook and a timeline for implementing them. Revisit your list afterward and reassess your level of compassion fatigue. Note the strategies that work best for you so you can rely on them as needed.

Professional strategies	Example
Create a boundary between work and home.	Stop or limit bringing paper-work home.
Change or lighten caseload/ workload.	See fewer cases until you're feeling better.
Schedule time off.	Take a vacation day, or make plans to take a trip on the next holiday.
Meet with a peer group (or establish one).	Start having Wednesday brown bag lunches with coworkers to check in.
Debrief with team or supervisor.	Ask your boss to meet and go over your workload.
Change work schedule.	Schedule difficult cases for the mornings, when you have more energy.
Physical strategies	Example
Get enough sleep.	Improve sleep hygiene (see chapter 4).
Eat a healthy diet.	Start a food diary (see chapter 4).
Exercise more.	Walk with friends during afternoon coffee break.
Get a checkup.	Call your doctor to schedule.
Psychological strategies	Example
Stress management	Practice yogic breathing (see chapter 4).
Time with support network/ family and friends	Plan a family dinner.
Compassion satisfaction (see page 38)	Reread notes and cards from people you've helped.

Compassion satisfaction counters compassion fatigue by grounding the work in meaning. When you engage in compassion satisfaction, you reinvigorate your compassion capacity by focusing on the things you've done right. You celebrate the contributions you've been able to make to others' lives and to your community as a whole. Compassion satisfaction focuses on strength and growth—your own and those of the people you've helped—rather than the painful side of the work you do. When you share success stories with a colleague, read a grateful note or e-mail from a former patient, or visit a relative who's thriving after you helped her through a tough time, you're treating yourself to compassion satisfaction. And you're inoculating yourself against compassion fatigue.

Exercise: Green Light, Yellow Light, Red Light

Once you've started deploying the techniques in this chapter to manage your emotions and defend against burnout and compassion fatigue, this exercise will help you stay on track by making small adjustments in the parts of your life that you're most concerned about. It's also helpful when you feel like *something* is going wrong, but you're not quite sure what.

The exercise is designed to help you see some of the behavior patterns that may be undermining you. Following the template on page 39, list in your notebook one or more aspects of your day-to-day life that are troubling you.

In the green light column, describe what that aspect of your life feels like when everything is at its best.

In the red light column, describe the worst-case scenario— what that aspect of your life is like when you're highly distressed and not functioning well.

In between, in the yellow light column, note one or two behaviors that start you in a negative direction, toward red.

Area of Concern	Green Light	Yellow Light	Red Light
Primary Relationship	Looks forward to spending quality time together, date once per week, able to effectively solve problems together, lots of affection	Forget to kiss good-bye and hello, don't ask about her day when I get home	Not connecting, spending very little time together; talking about surface level topics only, no dating, no touching
Friendships/ Social Life	Seeing friends regularly, keeping in touch via text or calls, frequently agree to social invitations	Delay answering texts from friends for hours, skip my regular Wednesday lunch with Sam two weeks in a row	Not socializing, spending most free time alone, lots of computer and TV in free time, people exhaust me
Anger	Rarely react to events with anger; anger is at levels that make sense, easily able to utilize time-out, easily able to address anger issues when calmed down	Stay up late watching TV and lose sleep, make excuses for raising my voice	Many anger events weekly, anger levels are often "10's," frequently acting out in anger, never using time-out
Performing Everyday Tasks	Notices triggers that lead to avoidance, can easily self-soothe, not tempted to avoid going out, consistently say yes to action and no to avoidance when urge to avoid comes up	Procrastinate weekly grocery shopping and just pick up things I desperately need, stop meditating	In full avoidance mode, going out only to work, ordering in food, no effort to notice triggers to avoidance

The behaviors you list in the yellow light column are warning signs to watch out for so you can reverse course. And they will help you develop strategies to reverse direction. For example, if you've turned down several social obligations over the course of a week, which you know is a yellow light behavior for you, you might say yes to the next three invitations from friends. If you notice you forgot to kiss your wife good-bye this morning, you can plan to spend extra time in greeting her when you get home.

Revisit this exercise as needed to manage not only the emotional symptoms of secondary trauma but any of the symptoms discussed in this book. And you can use the exercises found throughout the book to reverse any yellow light behavior.

Jamal's Story

Jamal works as an emergency room physician in a large metropolitan area. He's always loved his job, which is sometimes very intense, and other times slow and methodical. His coworkers are professional and caring. In the last few years, Jamal has noticed that being present with patients who are in pain is taking an increasing toll. He occasionally feels overwhelmed with intense emotions that cause his thinking to become muddled. But he's always been able to shake himself out of that state, and when it happens he makes sure to increase his self-care during his days off.

Most recently, a change in leadership at his hospital brought adjustments in staffing to save money. Over several months Jamal noticed himself complaining more often about the changes in working conditions and the lack of support from the hospital administration. When family members of his patients became emotional, Jamal would ask the nurse to take care of them, and he would leave the exam room. As his attitude about his job became more and more negative, Jamal became more easily irritated by patients. He spent less time with them. When other staff members came to him with problems, Jamal felt unable to cope with their emotions and would try to end the conversation quickly. Soon Jamal dreaded going to work and counted the hours of each shift.

On his days off Jamal became less and less inclined to participate in social activities. His wife tried to gently point out the changes she'd noticed, but he became upset, so she dropped the subject. Exhausted, Jamal spent most of his off time playing video games or watching TV. Sometimes he called in sick to avoid his job. He kept to himself while on duty. The situation came to a head one day when Jamal snapped at a nurse, who reported the incident to her supervisor. A meeting was called, and Jamal was confronted about his behavior by his own direct supervisor, another doctor.   »

« Very angry at first, Jamal told his boss that the staff was over-reacting. But his boss's caring concern got through to Jamal, and he broke down, admitting that he hadn't been acting like himself. Jamal's supervisor had some helpful suggestions to put him on a healthier track, encouraging him to use his employee assistance program (EAP) benefits (such as a referral to a therapist), limit his overtime hours, and get a physical exam to rule out any health issues. That night Jamal went home and had a long talk with his wife. He committed to getting help and returning to the person he used to be. Jamal knew accepting help and feedback from others was a necessary first step to his self-care journey.

Practicing and Tracking

Everything you're really good at, you have had to practice first. And you probably didn't feel competent at the skill until you had lots of practice under your belt. The same will be true of the strategies you use to cope with your emotional symptoms. This tracking worksheet will help you see which strategies you're good at and which will need more practice. And the more you use it, the more you'll be able to track how your skills are improving.

Start by deciding which symptom to focus on; we'll choose anger for this example. Copy the chart into your notebook, listing the symptom, the frequency at which it occurs, and how distressing it usually makes you feel. Then decide what strategy you're going to try; in this case, it's a time-out. Decide on a time frame for practicing the strategy—two weeks is a good length to start with. Note how often the symptom occurs, and each time rate how distressed you feel after you apply the chosen strategy. You'll see how well your self-care plan is working. A new skill will likely require more practice, and the worksheet will allow you to see incremental progress that you otherwise might not notice.

Date: *6 Oct.*

Symptom or Behavior: *Anger = yelling at home and work*

Beginning Frequency: *Daily at home; at least twice a week at work*

Baseline Distress (1-10): *8*

Strategy Used: *Time-out when I feel the urge to yell*

Where: *Work and home*

Practice Time Frame: *2 weeks*

Symptom or Behavior Frequency:_____

Ending Distress (0-10):_____

Outcome Notes: *After 2 weeks of practice, I am not yelling at work and yelled only twice at home*

Cultivating Change

Change isn't always easy. But as you move forward through this book, here are three general principles you can employ to increase your odds of success:

Deal with one issue at a time. When we try to fix too many things at once, we tend to get overwhelmed and give up before we've fixed anything. For example, some fascinating research found that most diets fail because the dieter is trying to change too many behaviors. What are the odds anyone can change twenty-six different bad eating habits in one go? But imagine tackling each of those habits one at a time. Sounds much more doable, doesn't it? Each small successful change boosts our confidence, building momentum that helps us achieve the next one.

Start small. Imagine a woman who wants to get in better shape and decides walking is the way to go. She puts on her sneakers one morning and starts strong, only to find herself a half mile from her home, exhausted. The next day the idea of going walking again sounds horrible, so she talks herself out of it. Thus begins a failure cycle.

As a counterexample: In a workshop I conducted some years ago, I spoke with a woman who wanted to exercise more. She said she wanted to walk for two miles a day. I asked what the odds were out of one hundred, that she would walk two miles every day that week. The answer she gave was 10 percent. I asked, "How about one mile?" The answer was 50 percent. When we got to a quarter mile, she told me her mailbox was about a quarter mile from her front door, and she felt 100 percent certain she could walk there once a day. Her aim may have been to walk two miles, but she began the journey by setting an achievable goal that she could build on later. When you decide to employ a new skill to manage your symptoms of secondary trauma, set a goal that you can reach with 90 to 100 percent certainty. And if you don't reach it, go smaller. If you fall off the horse, get right back on a smaller horse until you have regular success.

Go slow. Once you feel comfortable with your new skill, continue practicing it for two or three more weeks before you increase the frequency or duration or try to build another new habit. You'll not only build more competency, you'll enjoy the sense of accomplishment. Celebrate that you're working on something new, learning, and growing. Take time to be proud of yourself!

Imagine being in a grocery store and turning a corner to go down the canned beans aisle only to witness a mother yank her young son away from a display area, angrily reprimand him, and swat him hard on his bottom. If you believe spanking children is wrong, you might become outraged, then proceed to give a look of disapproval to the mother. On the other hand, if you believe children need strict discipline, you might be satisfied by what you see and smile at the mother.

Learning about the specifics of your value system can be an extremely beneficial exercise in self-awareness. Imagine that the person witnessing the mother and child was struggling with secondary trauma. If their value system was opposed to corporal punishment, the scene might have seemed violent and become a trigger for emotional symptoms like anger or sadness. On the other hand, someone who doesn't view that type of discipline negatively might not have been affected despite their secondary trauma. So understanding your value system can help you identify scenarios that might be problematic during your secondary trauma recovery.

When we violate our own values, we tend to feel guilty, which could trigger emotional symptoms if you've been impacted by secondary trauma. Copy the chart on pages 48–49 into your notebook, and fill it out to examine how your behavior and your emotional symptoms might be conflicting with your value system. Note which instances are most upsetting to you, then target your self-care plan to manage those symptoms. Return to the worksheet every so often to see how you're improving.

Value	Congruent Behavior at Work	Behavior Violation at Work	
Honesty	Work hard for every hour I'm paid for	Goof off playing solitaire instead of working	
Respect	Listening to ideas in staff meeting and allowing them to discuss them	Having a dismissive tone in meetings when someone suggests something I think is not workable	
Kindness	Checking in with coworkers to see how they are doing	Answering e-mails curtly, with only one or two words	

	Congruent Behavior in Relationships	Behavior Violation in Relationships	Emotion You Feel When Violating
	Letting my wife know when something is bothering me	Not answering truthfully when she asks how I'm doing	Sadness
	Slowing myself down when we are having an argument and really listening to her concerns	Yelling at the kids when they haven't done their chores	Anger
	Participating in a game my children chose because they want to teach me how to play	Insisting my family go to the restaurant of my choice and never letting them choose	Anger

Value	Congruent Behavior at Work	Behavior Violation at Work	
Honesty			
Respect			
Kindness			
Appreciation			
Dependability			
Service			
Trust			
Maturity			

	Congruent Behavior in Relationships	Behavior Violation in Relationships

Exercise: Charting Your Self-Care Plan

Each of the symptom-based chapters in this book (chapters 2 through 4) will conclude with a discussion of your self-care plan for the symptoms covered in that chapter. The details of your plan will be up to you. Choose the practices that seem most relevant after reading the chapter, trying the exercises, and reviewing the information you've collected in your notebook.

Self-care is about being a better, happier, healthier version of yourself. It means choosing to act in ways that support and improve your health and overcoming habits and behaviors that make you miserable. Addressing your secondary trauma symptoms with self-care will require making changes, and that's not always easy. The worksheet on page 51 will help you craft a self-care plan by identifying the areas where you're most ready to make a change.

Copy the chart into your notebook, and determine the stage you're currently in for each change you'd like to institute.

Self-Care Plan*

Area of Change	Specific Self-Care Strategies	Resources Needed	Which stage of change am I in?
Anger	Learn my triggers	Feeling triggers worksheet	Preparation
Anger	Practice time-outs	Keep sneakers at work to go walking when I'm feeling mad	Contemplation

*Based on Prochaska and DiClementi (1998).

The first stage of change is **precontemplation**: You don't see a need to make a change, at least in the next six months.

The second stage is **contemplation**. At this point, you see the negative consequences of the behavior you want to change. It's likely that any trauma symptom that's bothering you will fall into this stage or higher.

The third stage is **preparation**. At this point, you're planning, preparing, and gathering resources.

The fourth stage is **action**. In this stage, you're actively practicing new behaviors, seeking support, and developing effective self-care strategies for the change you want to make.

The fifth stage is **maintenance**. In this stage, you've kept up the change for more than six months, and you have resources in place to keep progressing and supporting the healthy behavior.

Use this chart to record each self-care plan that you develop. Update it as the components of your plan move from contemplation to action to maintenance.

Your Self-Care Plan

In this chapter, we saw that secondary trauma can have powerful emotional symptoms. Not everyone who's impacted by secondary trauma shows the same symptoms. But whatever feelings you are struggling with on your journey toward healing, you can learn to handle your emotions in a positive way.

Begin by understanding that emotions aren't good or bad in and of themselves. It's how we address them that can be positive or negative. When you experience an emotional flare-up, review what happened and assess whether you responded in an unhealthy way by escalating, avoiding, or converting your feelings. Review the strategies that you can use to manage your emotions instead.

Learn your triggers. Use the list on page 27–28, and the feeling triggers worksheet on page 30, as often as needed to identify what's triggering your symptoms. Anticipate or prepare for your triggers as best you can.

Manage your emotions with techniques like taking a time-out for anger and following an "opposite-to-emotion" strategy for sadness.

Be alert for symptoms of exhaustion and burnout. Read about getting restful sleep and easing stress in chapter 4.

Ease the struggle against negative emotions and burnout by employing the ACT exercise on page 35.

Regenerate your empathy when feeling compassion fatigue, referring to the list on page 37.

Discover your yellow light behaviors with the self-awareness exercise on page 39. Be alert for these behaviors, and use the exercises throughout this book to manage them.

See how well you're learning new skills by tracking your successes with the worksheet on page 43.

Learn the three principles of cultivating change and keep them in mind as you manage and heal all your secondary trauma symptoms.

Examine your value system, which is affected by your behavior, with the exercise on page 46.

Use the chart on page 51 to record your self-care plan and stages of change.

Takeaways:

+ Feelings can become triggers that become related to the trauma.

+ Feelings come from our thoughts that result from our reaction to events.

+ Anger, sadness, and hopelessness are common feelings related to trauma.

+ We have four basic strategies to deal with emotions: escalation, avoiding, converting, or managing them.

+ Knowing the triggers to any emotion can help us determine effective strategies to intervene with them.

+ Burnout and compassion fatigue are separate issues that can be related to secondary trauma.

+ Recognizing our signs of burnout and compassion fatigue are important to devising a plan to reverse their effects.

CHAPTER 3
Your Thoughts

Imagine you're in a meeting at work, and each team leader is pitching a new marketing plan. Two colleagues have already shared their presentations, and each of them emphasized the contributions that their team members made to the project. Then your own team leader gets up to speak. He takes credit for ideas that you and your teammates came up with and gives absolutely no credit to you or anyone else.

You find yourself thinking, "He is always so self-absorbed." "What a slap in the face!" "That's the last time I trust him." As the day progresses, you ruminate about the incident, feeling more and more disgusted and resentful. We might illustrate what happened this way:

EVENT

Team Leader takes credit for your idea.

THOUGHTS

He is always so self-absorbed.

What a slap in the face!

That's the last time I trust him.

FEELINGS

Disgust and resentment

ACTION URGE

Withdraw

Ignore his e-mails

Refuse to give him feedback

We tend to think of our thoughts and our feelings as separate. But as the example shows, events in our lives trigger thoughts, which lead to feelings and then an urge to act. In other words, feelings follow thoughts.

In the last chapter, we learned how to manage our feelings, mitigating the powerful emotional symptoms of secondary trauma. In this chapter, we're moving upstream from our feelings, to explore the thinking that gives rise to uncomfortable emotions. When we become aware of our thoughts and learn to intervene with them, we have a chance to break this event-to-action chain before our emotions overwhelm us. We'll examine ways that you can **distance** yourself from troubling thoughts, to loosen their hold on you. Then we'll learn to **examine** those thoughts and identify the distorted ways of thinking that can arise from secondary trauma. Finally, we'll discuss **reframing** your thoughts, to replace a negative inner voice with positive thinking.

Secondary Trauma Changes How You Think

Trauma can influence how you think as well as how you feel. As you seek to understand what happened and what it means, your thinking about the traumatic event and anything related to it may become progressively negative or distorted.

For example, Susan, a patrol officer, responded to several domestic battery calls. In each case the victim was highly emotional, making it difficult for Susan to get a clear story. A homicide detective contacted her a week later to get more details related to the death of someone Susan had interviewed. Soon after, Susan began imagining a wide range of potential criticisms from her department about her abilities. She decided she must have made a mistake, that she was a disappointment to her department, and that she'd been fooling herself thinking she was a good cop. Even after the detective interviewed her and said she'd done everything according to procedure, Susan continued to be self-critical and negative about herself and the job.

There are multiple ways our thinking can become distorted in the aftermath of trauma. Be on guard for these glitches in your thinking habits:

False explanations for lost memories. When someone witnesses a traumatic incident, it's not unusual for their memories to be incomplete. Because of the way the brain encodes trauma information, some details may be harder to access than regular memories. But attempts to explain those memory gaps can lead to erroneous and upsetting conclusions. For example, after the Las Vegas shooting in October 2017, I heard many survivors conclude that their missing memories were due to their brain trying to shield them from terrible things they'd seen. Trauma survivors sometimes come to believe they did something horrible or illegal during a memory gap. They may decide that something bad happened to them that they can't recall or feel that they're weak because they can't remember the entire narrative. None of those explanations are likely to be true. But taking stock in them can be greatly distressing for someone coping with secondary trauma.

Negative beliefs. Both direct trauma and secondary trauma can impel you to develop negative beliefs about yourself, others, or the world. You may see yourself as constantly victimized and powerless. You might think of yourself as broken, inadequate, weak, or pathetic. You might conclude that other people cannot be trusted, that friends and family won't be there for you, that they consider you a burden. You might have bad thoughts about the safety of your environment or the world in general. You might come to see the world as so hostile, you find malignant intent in even the most innocuous actions of others.

Exaggerated blame. As you try to make sense of a traumatic incident, exaggerated blame of yourself or of others can creep into your thinking. Deciding that someone is to blame, even if it's yourself, helps create predictability. You feel that you can prevent the traumatic event from recurring by changing your behavior or avoiding the responsible party. Of course, it makes sense to honestly assess any factors that contributed to a traumatic event and for responsible parties to be held accountable. But blame that's misplaced, exaggerated, or unfounded won't yield positive results. Instead, emotional reactions like fear, anger, and shame, along with other distressing emotions, will begin to surface.

Thoughts lead to feelings, and these distorted thinking styles can leave you so flooded by unpleasant emotions that it may seem like you don't have any positive feelings at all. The good news is you can learn to identify distorted thoughts. But to examine your thoughts you'll need to step back from them.

You Are Not Your Thoughts

Imagine yourself at an art gallery, viewing a large painting. If you stand just an inch away from the canvas, you won't have a real sense of what the painting depicts. You'll see the globs of color and pigment that are directly in front of your eyes, but you'll have no way of knowing whether the whole image is a vase of flowers, a pastoral meadow, or an abstract assemblage of lines and shapes. It's the same with our thoughts: When we hold them close, it's difficult to examine them. When we place some distance between us and our thoughts, it becomes easier to understand them and to intervene when they're not useful.

As you turn your attention toward your own thinking, it's important to remember that you are not your thoughts. If trauma has led you to adopt negative beliefs, exaggerated blame, or other forms of distorted thinking, that doesn't make you a bad person. In the last chapter, we noted that emotions like anger are not "bad" in themselves; it's how we respond that can be positive or negative. Similarly, feelings of shame or blame about your thoughts will make it harder for you to understand them. A thought is a changeable phenomenon. It's not who you are.

We can turn to acceptance and commitment therapy (ACT) to help us separate ourselves from our thoughts. It's a therapeutic approach that encourages what's called **cognitive defusion**: developing a relationship with your thoughts, even the troubling ones, that's open, curious, and interested. This makes it easier to spot and reject distorted thinking.

As an example, you might have the thought, "I'm not good enough at my job." This causes you to feel discouraged and weak, which causes you to avoid asking for a raise or a promotion or taking credit for the work you do. But suppose you approach that thought with curiosity: "Why do I think that about myself?" You might realize that you're blaming yourself for mistakes you didn't actually make, like Susan the patrol officer in the example discussed earlier.

Here are some powerful ACT techniques you can try to help separate and examine your thoughts:

De-literalizing language. Ever had an experience where you used a word so many times, it seemed to lose its meaning? This defusion technique emphasizes that phenomenon as a way to take power away from words that hurt us. For example, ACT therapists will often conduct the Milk, Milk, Milk exercise first outlined by Titchener in 1916. First a patient considers different implications of the word *milk*: milking a cow, a glass of milk, the sound of milk being drunk, and so on.

Then the patient repeats "milk" over and over, until they are just hearing it as a sound, not seeing the glass or any sensory images. Doing this helps us realize that words are merely symbols, and we don't have to get overly attached to them. Try it with neutral words like *milk*, then move on to the negative words that you inflict on yourself, like *loser* and *failure*.

Taking the wheel. With this defusion metaphor, you imagine yourself as a bus driver and your thoughts as passengers on the bus. The passengers want to tell you what to do and where to go, and generally you comply with them to keep them quiet. But you are in the driver's seat. You can choose to slow down, have conversations with the passengers, or even kick someone off the bus if you need to. When troubling thoughts become hard to manage, bring this image to mind.

Resisting phishing. When someone sends you a phishing e-mail, they try to get you to respond quickly and rashly by presenting you with bogus, emotionally loaded information. They're baiting you, "phishing" for personal details like a password or account number. But if you examine the message critically, the fakery becomes evident. If we approach a troubling thought as if it were a phishing attempt, we can notice how it might hijack our emotions and lead us to unhealthy feelings and actions.

One way to better understand your thoughts is to keep a log of events that lead to strong feelings, then list the thoughts you had at the time. Often this exercise reveals situations in which you get "stuck"—repeating an unhealthy pattern again and again, probably because of thoughts that perpetuate the "stuck" action. Here's an example of a log filled out by a single woman who recently went through a divorce.

Situation	Feelings	Thoughts
Who was there? What happened? When did this occur? Where were you?	*List all feelings related to the situation. Rate feelings 0 to 10.*	*What was going through your mind? List any thoughts or images.*
Thursday, driving to work, heard a love song on the radio when changing stations and started crying.	Sad (8) Lonely (10)	No one will ever ask me out; I am a loser. Imagined myself old and alone.

As she filled out the worksheet and examined her thoughts, the woman realized that every time something reminded her of her failed relationship, she would tell herself things that perpetuated her feelings of sadness and loneliness. Examining those thoughts, she determined that the next time she felt those feelings coming on, she could counter them with positive assertions: "I have amazing friends who are there for me," "I'm fortunate I have a challenging career," and "When I'm ready to date, I will try again."

When you find yourself experiencing the same emotional response again and again, copy the worksheet into your notebook, and use it to discover the thoughts that are keeping you stuck.

Exercise: Spotting Distorted Thoughts

Much of our response to trauma is a search for explanation. We want to make sense of why the traumatic event happened, to make us feel more in control of our lives. This is part of the healing process, but if we're not vigilant about it, we might make some wrong conclusions or erroneous assumptions. If I tell myself, "Bad things always happen to me," I'll end up feeling entirely differently than if I tell myself, "Sometimes bad things happen to me, but most of the time my life is very good," or "Bad things don't happen to me any more frequently than they do to others."

The following is a list of common types of distorted thinking that you should be on guard against. Copy the list into your notebook, and rate how frequently you engage in each of them (never, rarely, occasionally, sometimes, or often). As you get better at examining your thoughts, repeat the assessment to see how your thinking style has changed.

Black-and-white thinking. Characterizing a situation in absolutes, with words like *everyone, never, always,* and *none,* leaving no possibility for exception or nuance.

Examples: I will never get this done.
Positive counterexample: Even if I don't finish, the work I've done so far is valuable.

Disqualifying the positive. Discounting someone's positive feedback and refusing to accept praise.

Examples: He compliments everyone.
Positive counterexample: I'm really proud that my hard work was noticed.

Amplifying the negative. Overly focusing on the negative aspects of a situation, even if overall things clearly went well.

Examples: I stuttered during the first two minutes of my speech (even though the rest went extremely well and I received accolades).
Positive counterexample: I flubbed at the beginning, but once I got going I really gave a good speech.

Overgeneralization. Using one small detail to paint an inaccurate bigger picture.

Examples: I got upset with my children this morning so I'm a terrible mother.
Positive counterexample: I lost my temper this morning, but that was an exception. Nobody's perfect.

Mind Reading. Deciding that you know what someone else is thinking, feeling, or going to do, without confirming the truth with them.

Examples: I know he doesn't love me.
Positive counterexample: He doesn't seem to be enjoying our vacation . . . I'm going to ask what's bothering him.

Fortune-telling. Drawing a conclusion about the future with very little evidence to support it.

Examples: I know the boss is going to fire me because he's in a really bad mood today.
Positive counterexample: I'm going to ask around and see if anyone knows why the boss is so upset.

Should-ing on yourself or others. Applying an unwarranted imperative, a "should" or a "must," to yourself or another person.

Examples: I must do my best today.

Positive counterexample: I'll try to do my best today and accept whatever that brings.

Personalization. Taking something personally even though many other factors are involved.

Examples: She's late because she just doesn't like spending time with me.

Positive counterexample: She told me how much she was looking forward to our lunch, so something must be holding her up.

Control fallacy. Acting as if you're somehow in charge of everything . . . or in control of nothing.

Examples: I have to show my supervisor that she's being too lenient on her assistant.

Positive counterexamples: I don't agree with her hiring decision, but it doesn't affect me.

Fallacy of fairness. Assuming that everyone in the world understands and agrees to abide by the same system of rules. Breaking those rules is considered "unfair."

Example: Why is someone parking in the spot that I always park in?

Positive counterexample: I should have gotten here sooner if I wanted that parking spot.

Labeling. Applying a sweeping generalization using emotionally loaded words to describe yourself or someone else.

Examples: I'm so nervous in meetings; I'm a total loser.

Positive counterexample: Large groups make me uncomfortable—I'll sit with someone I know so I'll be more relaxed.

I Think, Therefore I DO

As discussed at the beginning of the chapter, events trigger thoughts, which lead to feelings, which lead to actions, like a row of tumbling dominos. We call this the "event-to-action" sequence. But just because you've had a particular thought, that doesn't mean the behavior *must* follow. You can stop the next domino before it falls over.

When we move from a thought to a feeling and then to an action, we can think of the action as having two components. First you feel an "action urge," and then you perform the action itself. Imagine being outside doing yard work on a warm day. You notice that you're feeling thirsty. An urge to go inside to get a drink arises. But that doesn't mean you immediately act on that urge. Maybe you decide to finish mowing a last patch of grass. Maybe you gather all your garden tools so you can carry them to the shed on your way to the house. But as you delay, the urge gets stronger and stronger. Eventually you break off from your gardening to go get a drink. Once you take that action, the urge goes away.

This same scenario plays out in countless ways for all of us on a daily basis. Most of our event-to-action sequences are quite functional, even mundane. But when the sequence is not healthy, we examine the components and make a change.

Imagine you're a mental health therapist working with trauma survivors. Your work has become more intense lately, and you notice some avoidance behavior on your part: When a patient starts a session with small talk, you allow it to continue long into the therapeutic hour, rather than redirecting the conversation toward active trauma work. You feel more and more guilty about doing this as the week progresses.

If we plug that into the event-to-action sequence, it would look like this:

Event

Trauma patient session

Thought

This work is too intense. I can't handle it.

Feelings

Anxious, overwhelmed

Action Urge: Avoidance

Action: Indulge in small talk

When you meet with your peer supervision group, a colleague admits he's been doing the same thing. As you discuss it, you realize the action urge of avoidance is natural, but you don't have to indulge in it. You consider the thoughts and feelings you've been experiencing and decide to try to change the sequence, introducing a new thought:

Event

Trauma patient session

New Thought

This is important work. It takes intense concentration.

Feelings

Determined, less anxious.

Action Urge: Slow down and re-center myself.

Action: Review the patient's treatment plan and recommit to it.

When an action or behavior isn't what you want, examining the thought behind it and substituting a new one can change the result. In this example, reminding herself of the importance of her work helped the therapist reduce her anxiety. When tempted to avoid the challenging aspect of her job, she reminded herself of the treatment plan she and her patient were meant to be following.

Breaking the link between thoughts and behaviors in this way may take repeated attempts, but it's an effective strategy. This is especially important when recovering from trauma, which can cause us to develop habits that feel more reactive and automatic. Use the event-to-action sequence to analyze the behaviors you want to change, and examine the thinking behind them. Then see what happens if you insert a new thought into the sequence.

Mindfulness is a contemplative practice that teaches us to slow down, center ourselves, and become more aware of our thoughts, feelings, and experiences. Mindful meditation is a particularly useful strategy for distancing from your thoughts. Begin by practicing the technique daily for just a few minutes at a time. Once you're familiar with the practice, try using mindful meditation to separate from troubling thoughts and calm yourself when your emotions are running high.

1. **Begin by sitting comfortably** (or lying on your bed, if possible).

2. **Close your eyes.** Breathe naturally. Notice the sounds and sensations around you without focusing concentration on them.

3. **As your thoughts arise and vie for your attention,** let each one fade out on its own, without giving it any energy. Try one or more of these visualizations:

   o Imagine lying on the grass in a beautiful meadow. See your thoughts float by one by one on the clouds above you.

   o Picture your thoughts going past on train cars. Hear the clack-clack of the rails. Watch each get smaller and smaller in the distance.

   o Envision your thoughts going by on a very long conveyor belt. Let each one hold your attention for just a few seconds before it passes.

   o Imagine sitting on the bank of a peaceful stream in autumn. Picture your thoughts as leaves, floating past you and drifting downstream.

○ See your thoughts written on balloons that you release one by one. Watch each float up into the sky and out of sight.

Exercise: How Effective Are Your Actions?

We've discussed how thoughts trigger feelings, which trigger actions, and how inserting a new thought can change the sequence, bringing about a healthier action. But when recovering from secondary trauma, it's not always clear where to start. And as mentioned at the end of chapter 2, change is easier if we don't try to change everything at once.

Sometimes it's helpful to evaluate your actions and behaviors in terms of how effective they are, rather than how "healthy" they are. Use that less emotionally loaded term when trying to assess which of your behaviors to focus on, and these three questions:

Does this action give me what is really best for me in the short term?

Does it address the emotions that caused it?

Will it bring positive consequences that align with my long-term goals?

Copy the following worksheet into your notebook to keep a record of the behaviors you're evaluating.

Action	Emotion	Short-term Effective?	Deal with Emotion?	Long-term Effective?	Need to Change?
Yelling	Anger	Yes—people leave me alone.	No—I still feel angry after.	No—I want to be close to others, not push them away.	Yes
Time-out	Anger	Yes—I get a chance to re-center.	Yes—I feel calmer and can catch thinking distortions.	Yes—I don't do any harm to my relationships.	No—this is working well.

GO DEEPER:
Mindful Breathing

Earlier we discussed a mindful meditation technique ("Watching Your Thoughts Go By," page 70). Mindfulness is a practice that can include not only meditation but prayer, journaling, yoga exercises, and many other activities. One can also practice mindfulness in a more general sense by learning to focus and attend to the present moment and detach from thoughts, feelings, and past experiences. Research has found that mindfulness techniques are effective in improving depression, anxiety, bad moods, emotional regulation, immune system functioning, chronic pain, positive emotional activity, and the ability to recognize negative thoughts.

If you want to explore mindfulness more deeply, a good first step is to practice mindful breathing.

1. **Take a deep breath and notice the sensation.** What is the temperature of the air as it enters your nose? Can you feel the air as it moves down into your lungs? Can you feel your lungs expand? Does the breath go all the way to the lower lobes of the lungs?
2. **Exhale, and notice all the sensations that follow.** Can you take a deeper breath? What does a shallow breath feel like? Can you slow your breathing down? How does that feel?
3. **Repeat** for as long as you like.

This type of mindful breathing can help center and calm you down. Try practicing it daily, so you can call on it when you need to calm your thoughts.

Answering Socrates

Learning to intervene with your thinking has been part of philosophical discussions for centuries. Indeed, the famed Greek philosopher Socrates wrote extensively of the importance of understanding and changing one's thinking when it's not accurate or useful. The questions in this exercise are based on several of the thinking exercises that Socrates developed to help his followers become more aware of their thoughts.

To examine a possibly troublesome thought, answer the questions in your notebook, and flag the answers that seem to give you the most insight into the thought you're examining. Note the ways in which the thought is distorted, untrue, or unhelpful . . . or accurate, positive, and useful.

- What is the situation in which the thought occurs?

- What am I thinking/imagining when the thought arises?

- What makes me believe this thought is true?

- What makes me believe this thought is not true or not completely true?

- What is a different way to look at the issue?

- What is the worst thing that could happen in relation to this thought? What would I do in response?

- What is the best that could happen?

- What will most likely happen?

- What will happen if I keep telling myself this same thought?

- What might happen if I change my thinking?

- What would I tell a friend (choose a specific person) if this happened to him/her?

Reframing Your Thoughts

Once we know how to distance ourselves from our thoughts and then examine and test them, it's time to intervene . . . to **reframe** our distorted or unhealthy thoughts to help us change our feelings and actions. We've touched a bit on this already, when we introduced a new thought into the event-to-action sequence earlier. In this exercise, you'll focus on replacing a specific negative or distorted thought that's troubling you with a healthy, balanced thought.

Confronting your thoughts this way by rewriting them on paper will train you to do the same thing in real time, in your head, when you catch an unhelpful thought arising.

Copy the following chart into your notebook. List the events that trigger your secondary trauma symptoms. For each event, write down thoughts that you experienced as best as you can remember them. Then write a more balanced, accurate, helpful thought to replace it with. (For extra practice, try adding balanced thoughts to the examples.)

Event	Original Thought	Balanced Thought
Seeing a fit person in the gym	I will never be in good shape.	I am consistently working out, and I can see progress compared to when I began.
At a party with a lot of people you don't know	I won't be interesting enough.	
Boss explains steps of project in detail	He must think I'm an idiot and need to be treated like a child.	
Hear fireworks that sound like gunshots	I am going to get shot at again.	

(Continued)

Event	Original Thought	Balanced Thought
Friend had to cancel dinner	I must have offended him.	
Struggled with a presentation at a staff meeting	Because I was uncomfortable, I will never get promoted.	
Wife had a bad day at work so she wasn't very talkative	She isn't talking much because I'm so boring.	
Get cut off on the freeway	He did that on purpose!	
Boss comments on how well you han- dled a cardiac call	He compliments everyone.	
Yelled one time during a very stressful day	I am always angry.	

Cora's Story

Cora began taking care of her mother, Sandra, after Sandra was assaulted in the parking lot of her workplace. Cora is the oldest of her siblings, has two children of her own, ages 15 and 12, and lives with her husband of 17 years. She works a part-time job in addition to caring for her family and mother.

Sandra experienced a head trauma in the attack as well as several broken bones and was put into a medically induced coma for three weeks afterward. She had multiple surgeries and was transferred to a rehabilitation hospital for physical and occupational therapy. As she recovered, Sandra recounted the details of her assault over and over in Cora's presence, to the doctors, nurses, and police. When it was time for Sandra to move back home, she called Cora, crying, telling her she was afraid the man who assaulted her was going to find her and "finish what he started."

Cora and her husband decided it made sense to move Sandra into their home, since she couldn't drive and would need help getting to and from doctor appointments. Cora transported her mother every day while juggling her work and family obligations. She began to notice her sleep was disrupted. The months wore on, with doctor appointments, more interviews by the police, and many conversations with her mother about her trauma. Cora became more irritable, exhausted, and discouraged and noticed she was regularly nervous anytime she was away from home. She had a hard time attending to her husband or her children. Sometimes she felt completely shut down, and other times she was so on edge that she flew off the handle over the slightest cause. »

» Two years after the attack, Cora's doctor became concerned with her twenty-five-pound weight gain and elevated blood pressure. As he asked Cora questions, the story tumbled out about her mother's assault, the court case, and how she felt. The doctor suggested she see his colleague, who could further assess her for secondary trauma. Cora thought the doctor hadn't heard her right—it was her mother who had been assaulted, not her. The doctor explained to her that hearing the story of her mother's assault over and over, and being her mother's caretaker, could cause her to have her own trauma response. She agreed to be evaluated for secondary trauma and began to assess how she had been impacted by exposure to her mother's trauma.

Exercise: Downward Arrow Technique

When you're having trouble reframing a difficult thought, the downward arrow technique can help. It's a simple but powerful exercise taken from cognitive behavioral therapy (CBT), an approach to mental wellness that emphasizes the way thoughts, feelings, and behavior impact each other. Begin with the thought you want to explore and ask yourself, "What is the meaning of that thought?" Repeat with each answer, continuing until you gain an insight into that thought. It may take three arrows, or it could take ten or more. You may gain a more positive, balanced thought, but the goal is to understand the original thought better.

You can perform the exercise out loud or silently in your mind. You may find it helpful to write your answers down in your notebook so you can remember the chain of questions and answers. Here's how the exercise might look:

No one can be trusted.

↓

What does that thought mean to you?

↓

People will let me down.

↓

What does that thought mean to you?

↓

That I will always hurt like I do now.

↓

What does that thought mean to you?

↓

That I cannot do anything to get better.

↓

What does that thought mean to you?

↓

That I've given up trying.

↓

What does that thought mean to you?

↓

I don't know what to do next.

↓

What does that thought mean to you?

↓

That I'm willing to get help.

↓

What does that thought mean to you?

↓

I'm more open to changing than I thought I was.

Exercise: Keeping a Thought Record

Another strategy that's used in CBT is to create a thought record, a log of occasions when your secondary trauma symptoms cause problems—and an examination and reframing of the thoughts and feelings that occurred. Copy the worksheet into your notebook, and fill it out when a trauma-related incident occurs. Fill in your thought record as close to the event as possible, while the details are fresh in your mind.

Event	I was at a restaurant with a friend when a busboy dropped a tray of dishes and I jumped.
Triggers	Loud noises; being around strangers
Vulnerabilities	I had a really bad morning at work and was already on edge.
Thoughts	I am broken.
Feelings	Fear 5 Embarrassment 8
Evidence your thoughts are accurate	It's been a year, and I still jump. No one else jumped but me. Restaurants bother me.
Evidence your thoughts are inaccurate	I was able to calm down pretty fast; I was able to make a joke about it. My friends still enjoy my company.

Healthy thought	I am actively working on myself, and I'm getting better at calming myself down.
Re-rate feelings	Fear 1 Embarrassment 2

Event: Record what happened, when, where, and who else was present.

Triggers: Did you notice any of your triggers (see chapter 2)?

Vulnerabilities: Did any circumstances make you more susceptible to reacting negatively?

Thoughts: What were the thoughts during and after the incident? What does that mean about you?

Feelings: List the emotions you felt, and rate each of them on a scale of 0 to 10 for intensity.

Evidence your thoughts are accurate: List any evidence that the thoughts you recorded are accurate.

Evidence your thoughts are inaccurate: List any evidence the thoughts you recorded are not true or not fully true.

Healthy thought: Write a healthy thought that is more accurate and more reflective of your awareness of your vulnerabilities and your triggers.

Re-rate feelings: List the same feelings as before, but re-rate the intensity from 0 to 10 based on your new, healthy thought.

Your Self-Care Plan

In this chapter, we explored the ways that our thoughts affect our recovery from secondary trauma. We began by looking at the **event-to-action** sequence, which shows how our thoughts lead to feelings, which lead to actions. Understanding our thoughts enables us to intervene in this sequence.

Start your plan by accepting that **you are not your thoughts**. Uncomfortable thoughts don't make you a bad person. Let go of any shame or blame about your thoughts, so you can understand them more easily.

Distance yourself from troubling thoughts by learning the **cognitive defusion techniques** of acceptance and commitment therapy (ACT), page 61. Discover the thoughts that are keeping you stuck with the exercise on page 63, and watch out for the distortions in thinking listed on page 64.

Use the **event-to-action sequence** to see how a different thought could yield a different action urge. Try **mindful meditation** to detach from your thoughts. **Mindful breathing** can calm you when you feel overwhelmed by troublesome thoughts or emotions.

Examine your thoughts by considering how effective they are and connecting them to actions and emotions with the worksheet on page 72. Test them with the questions on page 71.

Reframe unhealthy thoughts with healthy, balanced thoughts using the worksheet on page 75. Use the downward arrow technique to help you connect with balanced thoughts and deepen your understanding of underlying thoughts.

Use a **thought record** to examine your thoughts after a troubling incident and reframe them.

Use the chart on page 51, at the end of chapter 2, to record your self-care plan and stages of change.

Takeaways:

+ Secondary trauma changes how you think in many ways. Understanding these changes can help you improve your thoughts.

+ Cognitive defusion can aid you in separating yourself from your thoughts.

+ Most of us have some distortions in our thinking. Learning about the various distortions can help you catch them.

+ Meditation can be very useful in separating from your thoughts and healing from trauma.

+ Separating from your thoughts helps you examine and test them.

+ Unhealthy thoughts can be reframed or replaced with more positive ways of thinking, which will lead to healthier emotions and behaviors.

CHAPTER 4

Your Body

If you're recovering from exposure to secondary trauma, you may find that friends and family question how the trauma can cause physical symptoms. You yourself may be confused by this. After all, by definition, secondary trauma is an event that happened to someone else. If you weren't even present, how could it be affecting you physically?

The fact is, the mind and the body are connected in many ways. When you experience high stress at work, you might notice that your stomach has a knot in it, that your shoulders and neck feel stiff by the end of the day, or that you have a headache—all physical symptoms resulting from a psychological condition. Every time we have an emotional experience, our body reacts. When trauma happens, our body prepares to fight, flee, or freeze. Secondary trauma produces this effect when we're exposed to the details and imagery of a traumatic incident. Over time, a prolonged fight/flee/freeze reaction can affect our body in ways we might not connect to the initial trauma exposure. We can develop digestion problems, headaches, aches and pains, high blood pressure, even a lowered immune system that leads to more frequent seasonal colds and infections.

In this chapter we'll review how secondary trauma can manifest itself in your body. We'll learn some mind-body healing techniques. We'll pay special attention to sleep, one of the most important ways that your body heals and renews itself. And we'll discuss ways to improve your exercise and dietary habits, to build a strong foundation for healing.

What Secondary Trauma Can Do to Your Body

Trauma begins with an activation of the fear circuitry in the brain, primarily in an almond-shaped cluster of nerves called the amygdala. This activation triggers the release of specific chemical messengers, or neurochemicals, that affect all parts of your body to prepare you for danger. But sometimes it's hard for that area of your brain to understand when the danger is over. Our fear response evolved to protect us from predators and other obvious threats and isn't as good at judging if we're safe from other humans or modern-day hazards. In the case of secondary trauma, the line between threat and safety may be even less clear, since you experience the traumatic incidents through recounted details and images and not directly.

If your brain stays locked in survival mode, it keeps your body flooded with those fight-or-flight neurochemicals. And over the long term, this can affect your health in many ways. You might develop:

Cardiovascular problems. Chemicals released by your body during trauma increase your heart rate and dilate your blood vessels, to increase blood flow so you can respond to threats. Prolonged exposure can cause high blood pressure, inflammation of the circulatory system, and heart disease.

Muscular pain. When your fight-or-flight system activates, blood is pumped to the muscles to give you strength. If this effect doesn't shut down, muscles remain tense and cause neck and back pain, headaches, and migraines. The tension affects sleep and causes you to be hypervigilant, because your tense muscles feel like a signal that the environment is not safe.

Endocrine system problems. The endocrine system handles the release of chemical messengers into your bloodstream. When it continuously produces fight-or-flight chemicals, your immune system can be weakened, and you may be more vulnerable to endocrine-related disorders like diabetes, obesity, and chronic fatigue syndrome.

Gastrointestinal issues. When your fight-or-flight response is activated, your digestive system is essentially shut off, since it's not important for short-term survival. And if your brain doesn't switch back into safe mode, your digestive system may remain inhibited, leading to heartburn, gassiness, bloating, problems with appetite, diarrhea, constipation, nausea, and exacerbated symptoms of irritable bowel syndrome or Crohn's disease.

Reproductive health issues. Since the male and female reproductive systems are part of the endocrine system, it's not unusual for trauma to affect them. In men, trauma can depress testosterone levels, sperm production, and libido. For women, trauma can change menstrual cycles and decrease sexual desire and may create more premenstrual discomfort.

That may seem like an extensive list of health issues, but keep in mind that not everyone will experience all of those effects. And the good news is that the mind-body connection works both ways. When you exercise and eat a healthy diet, you'll not only strengthen your muscles and nourish your body, you'll sleep better, boost your mood, and relieve feelings of depression and anxiety. When you manage your thoughts and emotions and reduce your stress, you'll heal your immune system, your digestion may regulate, and other chronic diseases may ease. Our interconnected mind and body means we can address our health problems from two sides.

Long-Term Stress

Our body is set up to best deal with stress that has a distinct beginning, middle, and end. Unfortunately, modern life can expose us to stress that doesn't have such clear-cut boundaries. We may encounter **chronic stress**, which is unpredictable and has no definitive end point: poverty, dysfunctional relationships, difficult or dangerous jobs, and long-term health issues can all produce chronic stress. The resulting long-term release of hormones, especially a chemical called **cortisol**, has been found to contribute to many diseases and health problems, ranging from heart disease and some types of cancer, to a higher risk of accident or suicide. If you have both trauma and chronic stress, your cortisol system may be overactive. Healing the trauma and learning new skills to deal with your stress could enhance your life and repair your body.

Mind-Body Healing

Healing the mind involves the body, and healing the body involves the mind. They make up a connected system. So the techniques you've learned in earlier chapters of this book, to address trauma symptoms related to your thoughts and emotions, can help with the healing of your body, too. But specifically addressing the body allows the mind the best environment to heal. Keep these principles in mind as you work to bring both mind and body to good health:

Be aware of how your emotions affect your body. When you don't address troubling emotions in a healthy way (see chapter 2), your body can react in ways that lower the immune system. This can lead to catching a cold, the flu, or some other type of virus. Emotions and stress can also impact our sleep, cardiovascular health, digestion, muscle tension, appetite, and headaches. Anytime your secondary trauma produces strong emotional symptoms or stress, pay particular attention to your body and watch for a physical reaction. Take extra care that you're getting good sleep, exercise, and nutrition.

Assess your emotional state when you're feeling unwell. Conversely, when physical symptoms flare up, assess your emotional health. Do you need to work more on managing your feelings (chapter 2) or the thoughts that lead to them (chapter 3)?

Don't let emotional symptoms interfere with health maintenance. Strong emotions and stress can sometimes distract us to the point where we begin to neglect self-care. But while you're working on the psychological effects of secondary trauma, it's important to keep up with the activities that support your physical health, like eating right, getting good sleep, getting regular checkups, and taking medication as prescribed.

Exercise: Boosting Mind-Body Awareness

One way to touch base with the health of both mind and body is to conduct a mind-body scan. Here's how it works:

1. Begin by lying down, or sitting in a comfortable chair. Close your eyes and relax.
2. Check in with your mental activity. Notice the speed of your thoughts. Are they going by very fast? Are they sluggish?
3. Notice the nature of your thoughts. Are they largely negative? Positive? Neutral?
4. Then notice the content of the thoughts themselves. What are you actively thinking about today? Tasks that must be done? Things that happened yesterday? Stories from many years ago? Issues that may come up in the future?

5. Note your overall feeling state. What would you label these feelings? Are you comfortable with these feelings? Are they familiar? Do they make sense?

6. Next, turn your attention to your body. Start by focusing attention on your head. Do you feel any sensations or tension? Take note, focusing on that information for a few moments. Then move your attention to your neck, your shoulders, and slowly down your body. Scan each area for tension, stiffness, aches, restlessness, or any other sensation. Continue until you've scanned yourself from head to toe.

When you're finished, remain in place for a while and consider the data you collected about body and mind. Can you draw any connections? Remain curious about how your thoughts and your body might be signaling one another.

Once you've practiced the mind-body scan for several days, you may find it useful to make notes in your notebook to find patterns. For example, you might notice that when you think a great deal about future events, you get a knot in your stomach. Maybe the tension in your shoulders is increased when you feel irritated about work drama. Or you might notice you feel light and relaxed after you have had a pleasant interaction with your family. Learning to attend to these signals can help you identify sources of stress and sources of comfort.

Exercise: Tai Chi

Movement is extremely important to our overall well-being. Exercise causes a chemical response in the body that counters the effects of stress and trauma.

Tai chi is an ancient Chinese exercise practice that's performed as a series of slow, meditative movements. It can help reduce stress, enhance positive moods, increase energy, improve balance, and strengthen muscles. The breathing and meditative components of tai chi bring additional benefits that help with sleep, lower blood pressure, and improve immune functioning. Some older adults who practice it report that they have better balance, which reduces their risk of falls. It's a great low-impact exercise option if you're not used to a regular, intense workout.

To try it, look for classes in your area; gyms, senior centers, and community centers frequently offer tai chi classes for beginners.

Exercise: Yogic Breathing

Most of the time, we don't pay much attention to the quality of our breathing from one minute to the next. But you've probably noticed that when you're anxious or angry, you tend to breathe rapidly and shallowly. Yogic breathing is a way of countering feelings of anxiety or stress with a breath pattern that's slow and centering.

To practice yogic breathing, follow these steps:

1. Sit in a comfortable chair or lie down in bed.
2. Take a deep breath, letting your chest and belly rise, and picture the air going deeper and deeper into your lungs as you inhale.
3. Breathe out slowly, imagining the air emptying completely from your lungs.
4. Continue to breathe in and out, noticing the speed of your breathing, slowing it down while keeping your breaths deep.
5. Continue breathing at a comfortably slow pace until you feel relaxed and refreshed.

Practice this daily and use it as needed for stress reduction.

Amira's Story

Amira has worked at a domestic violence shelter for women and children for the last few years. She became passionate about this type of work because her own mother had been battered by her father, until she finally left him when Amira was nine years old. Amira could relate to the women she helped and was regularly praised by her supervisor and the clients for her caring and compassion.

Perhaps the most difficult part of her job was when a woman went back to her abuser, only to return to the shelter a few months later. Amira listened to story after story about emotional abuse, control, jealousy, property destruction, threats, and severe physical abuse. In one particular week, she admitted one woman who'd been hospitalized after her boyfriend shot her in the leg, another who came to the shelter with only the clothes on her back because her boyfriend wouldn't let her take a bag, and a woman who arrived from another state because she was afraid to go to a shelter in her own area. In each case Amira listened to their stories, helped connect them to services, assisted with temporary protection orders, and tried her best to help them get skills that might prevent them from returning to their abusers.

Over the last year, Amira began having frequent headaches. One day she woke with a different type of headache, which came with severe nausea and light sensitivity. When this happened a second time, she made an appointment with her family doctor. After questioning, Amira admitted to her doctor that she'd been sleeping poorly. She was having nightmares that combined her memories of her mother's ordeal with stories from women she met at the shelter. The doctor explained her headaches were possibly connected to her exposure to trauma. He told Amira that trauma experiences can affect the muscular system, which can cause muscle tension, spasms, and headaches. He recommended therapy and relaxation techniques, and they scheduled a follow-up appointment to check on her progress.

The Healing Power of Sleep

To say that sleep heals is a gross understatement: Sleep is absolutely essential for survival. Yet the World Health Organization has acknowledged sleep deprivation is an epidemic in all industrialized countries.

Here's what your life will be like if you regularly and consistently let yourself sleep at least eight hours per night:

Your overall health will be superior to those who do not sleep eight hours. You will have a more robust immune system, half the risk of cancer, less likelihood of developing Alzheimer's disease, a lowered chance of diabetes, less cardiovascular disease, and less chance of a stroke.

You'll probably lose weight. The hormones that regulate hunger and satiety will be better regulated, and your body will develop a healthier assortment of beneficial microbes that aid in digestion.

You'll have less depression and anxiety than your sleep-deprived counterparts.

You'll recover more quickly from exercise and surgeries, as our bodies more quickly repair themselves during sleep.

Your concentration at work will be superior to your sleepier coworkers. You'll make fewer mistakes and will also have a longer attention span and more energy, be less forgetful, and have better moods.

You'll do better in school or in any kind of learning environment. Sleep helps you consolidate memories, so you learn better when you sleep well.

You'll be in fewer crashes. One study that looked at car crashes before and after daylight saving time in the United States and Canada found a significant increase in crashes on the Monday in areas where residents lost one hour of sleep (Coren, 1996, cited in Myers, 2005).

Trauma can cause sleep disruption that falls into two broad categories:

Insomnia is an inability to maintain adequate sleep, despite giving yourself enough sleep time. There are two main types: sleep onset insomnia and sleep maintenance insomnia. In the first case, falling asleep is difficult, but once sleep comes, it's lasting. The second case occurs if you fall asleep fairly easily but then wake up in the night, or wake far too early in the morning, and can't fall back to sleep. It's possible to suffer from both types. According to sleep expert Matthew Walker (2017), founder of the Center for Human Sleep Science, trauma survivors are very likely to suffer from insomnia. This can include patchy sleep in which you wake up for brief times throughout the night, without remembering it the next day. It's possible to feel sleepy and fatigued without realizing that you didn't get adequate sleep.

Nightmares are emotionally disturbing, and they can be very disruptive to your sleep. You may develop sleep maintenance insomnia because it's difficult to fall back to sleep after an upsetting nightmare. Other times, anxiety about having a nightmare may cause sleep onset insomnia.

Understanding why we dream can help you cope with nightmares. But don't rely on a dream interpretation book to decode the meaning of your dreams. Each of us creates our own symbols that are recycled into the dreams we have. For example, if you were raised on a farm, you might find yourself on a farm in a dream, connected to feelings of contentment or happiness. If you've never been on a farm in your life, the setting would be unlikely to show up in a dream.

Researchers have found that dreams have significant functions in keeping us healthy. Among other things, they seem to help us explore the emotional themes of our waking life—an important concern for anyone coping with secondary trauma. Dreaming changes the chemicals in your brain, creating stronger levels of emotion than we experience when awake. It's as if dreams are an effort to work through emotions while we sleep, to decrease their impact when awake. This is why we often wake feeling better the day after a difficult experience.

Exercise: Your Dream Log

Keeping a dream log can help you see how your dreams and nightmares parallel what's happening in your life and can point to aspects of your secondary trauma you need to address. The idea is to document any dreams you remember, either when you wake in the morning or whenever you wake up after dreaming. It's best to use a separate, designated notebook for this exercise.

Important details to note in your log:

What were your feelings in the dream?

Who were the people or characters in the dream, and what do they symbolize for you (an enemy, an ally, a teacher)?

What actions did you take in the dream, and what might those symbolize?

Over time, as the same actions, feelings, and people show up in dreams, you will be able to figure out what they might mean for you—what message your dreams are giving you about something that's happening in your life. For example, if your dreams frequently involve strong feelings of anger or sadness, you may need to focus on those emotions with the techniques explained in chapter 1.

Note that not everything in your dreams will be connected to your trauma. Any important aspect of your waking life might be integrated into your dreams. Understanding your dreams can be a very involved process, beyond the scope of this book. Recurring nightmares may require the help of a therapist to uncover the source. To pursue the topic further, see Matthew Walker's book *Why We Sleep: Unlocking the Power of Sleep and Dreams* (Scribner, 2017).

Exercise: A Meditation for Better Sleep

If you have trouble falling asleep, a meditation exercise can help. Here's a simple method you can practice every night. Conduct your sleep hygiene routine first (page 97).

1. Lie on your bed in a comfortable position.
2. Turn your attention to your breathing. Notice your chest and stomach rising then falling with each breath. Breathe in and out. In and out.
3. When you're comfortable, take a deeper breath. Feel the air go down deeper into your lungs.
4. Breathe deeply. Slow down your breathing, and notice how it makes your whole body feel heavier, more deeply relaxed.
5. Continue to breathe at a slow and comfortable pace, and turn your attention to your feet. Feel the weight of the blanket on your feet, and feel the way your heels indent into the mattress.
6. Focus on any muscle tension or energy in your feet as you breathe, and push that tension out as you exhale. Grab that muscle tension or energy as you breathe in, then breathe it out of your body.
7. Turn your attention to your calves and thighs. Feel their weight. If there's any tension or energy in your calves and thighs, grab it with your inhaled breath, and exhale the tension out.

8. Continue to slowly work your attention up your legs, into your torso, your chest, your arms, and your neck and shoulders. For each area, scan for tension, and breathe it out with slow, deep breaths. Let all of the tension go out of your body, easily and completely.

9. Bring your awareness to your face and head. Soften the muscles throughout your face. Let your eye muscles go, release your jaw, feel your tongue become a puddle in your mouth. Continue to breathe deep and slow, releasing any tension each time you exhale.

10. Gather any thoughts in your mind left over from the day, and allow them to float away. (You can use the visualizations from "Watching Your Thoughts Go By" on page 70.)

Exercise: Blueprint for Better Sleep

When we consider the behaviors and habits that affect our ability to get deep, restful sleep, we're talking about sleep hygiene. Developing an effective **sleep hygiene** routine means eliminating anything that inhibits sleeping and creating a bedtime ritual that will efficiently signal the brain that it's time to sleep. Review the following list, and note which of these sleep hygiene practices are relevant and achievable for you. Copy them into your notebook to create a plan for better sleep.

Keep the bedroom dark. Even a bit of light exposure activates a gland in the brain that keeps us awake. Minimize any light exposure, including screen illumination from televisions, phones, clocks, and computers. Use curtains to block window light. A sleep mask may help, though not everyone finds them comfortable.

Avoid eating before bed. Our bodies will not fully relax until the food in our system is digested past a certain point. Institute a "no food for an hour before bedtime" policy, and adjust the stop time as needed.

Avoid exercise and activity right before bed. Exercise earlier in the day, which will help you sleep better (spend time outdoors if possible; daytime sun exposure helps regulate brain chemicals that enhance our sleep). But too much activity close to your sleep time can keep you awake.

Avoid caffeine in the evening, as well as alcohol and excess fluid intake. Some people are so sensitive to caffeine that they need to limit it to mornings only.

Avoid any activity in bed other than sleep or sex. Watching television, reading, using a laptop or phone, and other activities should be avoided before bed, since they'll make it harder for your mind to relax. This is especially true of emotionally loaded activities, like reviewing work e-mails or watching a disturbing program. And whatever the time of day, it's best not to do any of these in bed. You want your brain to associate your bed with sleeping only.

Avoid napping during the day, especially naps lasting longer than fifteen minutes.

Stick to a consistent bedtime. Go to bed within an hour of the same time nightly, to cue your body that it's time to sleep. Pick a bedtime that gives you more hours for sleeping than you need (eight hours, typically), so you won't feel anxious if you don't fall asleep right away. Keep to the same schedule on weekdays and on the weekend.

Keep your bedroom cool. Try setting the thermostat somewhere in the mid to low 60s to start, and adjust until you find the right temp for you.

Try changing your bedding. Everyone has different preferences; you may find that a different textured sheet or a new pillow makes a big difference for your sleep.

Construct a personal bedtime ritual. A habitual routine at bedtime, lasting 45 minutes to an hour, can be a powerful sleep inducer. You might start with a shower or bath, then adjust the bedroom environment (turn down the temperature, lower the lights, shut off electronics), then do the sleep meditation on page 96. The details are up to you, but once you find the right combination, stick to it every night.

Exercise: Collecting Sleep Data

Not sure what's keeping you from sleeping? You might try using one of the many electronic devices, and apps for your phone or smart watch, that monitor you while you sleep. Here are some data points to look for:

How much deep sleep versus light sleep are you getting?

How frequently do you wake in the night?

How many hours per night are you sleeping?

Do you keep to a strict sleep and wake time every day?

You address the results by applying sleep hygiene principles. For example, you may notice that your sleep is poorer if you have a late dinner or on days when you exercise after work. You may find that going to bed an hour late doesn't impact your sleep, but a later bedtime than that means you toss and turn for hours.

You can also discuss your sleep data with your doctor, who may refer you to a specialist to rule out any physical problems.

GO DEEPER:
What Is Your Body Telling You?

Our bodies are constantly sending us messages, but it can be a challenge to figure out what the message is. Train yourself to read the signals by reviewing these questions:

- Do you know the difference between your body signaling "I need more sleep" versus "I'm bored"?

- Do you know the difference between your body signaling "I'm hungry" versus "I'm eating to soothe my emotions"?

- Do you know the difference between your body signaling "I'm sore from exercising" versus "I'm injured"?

- Do you know the difference between your body signaling "I'm about to make a mistake" versus "I'm tense"?

- Do you know the difference between feeling an emotion versus feeling a physical need?

Answer these questions in your notebook, listing the differences between the signals where you can, and return to the questions as you pursue your recovery. Scan yourself at contrasting times (use the mind-body scan on page 89): after a particularly stressful day at work, during a relaxing day off, anytime you feel a strong emotion (positive or negative). Over time you'll become more and more informed about how your body speaks to you.

Becoming connected to your body will help you become more aware of your physical symptoms. Think of yourself as a scientist in your own life—curious, open, interested, and methodical. This exercise encourages you to explore the physical symptoms of your trauma individually, while at the same time looking for connections to other symptoms.

Copy the chart into your notebook, and fill in the details for each symptom you wish to explore.

Symptom: *Stomach knot*

Duration: *2 hours in the morning*

Intensity (1-10): *5*

Frequency: *Daily on workdays*

Factors: *Pressure? Work? Boss? Rushing? E-mails?*

Intervention: *Allow an extra 20 minutes to get to work*

Helped? *Yes*

Note any factors that may be contributing to the symptom. These could include places, people, tasks, another physical symptom, or anything that gives you stress. When the symptom recurs, cross off any factors that aren't applicable until you are down to one or two that are always present.

Once you identify a potential contributing factor, note down a way to change or avoid it. Repeat until you find a useful intervention. Include the symptom and intervention in your self-care plan at the end of this chapter.

Keep in mind there might be times you will need to consult with a doctor if a symptom persists no matter what intervention you try or becomes physically painful.

Exercise: Wheel of Health

This exercise explores your relationship with physical health and helps you visualize your health status.

The wheel of health includes eight different subcategories that combine to give you an overall view of your focus on health.

Copy the Wheel of Health into your notebook. The wheel divides your overall physical health into eight different sub-categories. Rate yourself in each, from 1 (minimal) to 10 (excellent).

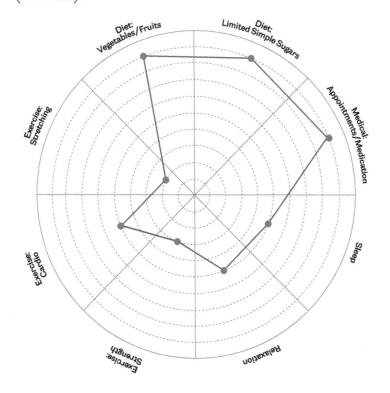

Diet: Vegetables/Fruits. How diligent are you about eating these healthy foods?

Diet: Limited Simple Sugars. How careful are you to avoid foods with added sugar?

Medical: Appointments/Medication. How well do you keep up with doctor appointments and prescribed medicine?

Sleep. How consistently do you get deep, restorative sleep?

Relaxation. Are you making sure to include downtime in your daily schedule?

Exercise: Strength. Are you regularly performing weight-bearing exercises like weight lifting?

Exercise: Cardio. Are you active enough for your heart rate and breathing to speed up?

Exercise: Stretching. Do you move your body through a full range of motion?

Connect the ratings for a visual picture of your health, showing the strongest and weakest factors, as in the example.

Choose a less-developed area to work on. In the example, this person might decide to work on stretching to increase his balance and flexibility. He'll set a goal that will move him from his score of two to a score of three—perhaps to attend a tai chi class (see page 90) for several weeks. A small and actionable goal can move him up one step. Then he can set the next goal to move up another step, and so on.

Nourishing the Body and Mind

Nutrition is a complicated subject but an important one. Our diet is the direct source of our body's energy and so a vital subject for anyone healing from trauma. The food we eat not only fuels our recovery, it can have a significant impact on our mental state. For example, one study of people suffering from depression found that those who switched to a healthy diet (high in vegetables, fruits, whole grains, and lean meats) for just twelve weeks were less depressed and significantly happier than others who stayed on a diet high in processed foods (Jacka et al., 2017). Salty foods tend to dehydrate us, and as a result we feel more fatigued. Foods with high fat content raise our stress hormone levels and keep them high. Multiple studies have shown that people who eat diets high in sugar have many problems regulating stress, concentration, attention, and mood.

Here are some nutrition principles to keep in mind:

Nutrition is more than dieting. It seems like there's a surplus of quick-fix solutions to all our diet problems, but research shows that most weight-loss diet regimens are not sustainable. Most people will gain back any weight they lose—and more.

How, when, and where we eat can be as important as what we eat. For example, if you eat in too many locations—standing in your kitchen, on the couch in front of the TV, in your car, in bed—your brain becomes over-cued to eat, and you take in too many calories.

Know the basics. We're barraged with nutrition advice from all kinds of sources: fad diet ads, news stories, friends and family. But the basic principles of good nutrition haven't changed much over the years. The President's Council on Sports, Fitness, and Nutrition recommends these eight goals:

- Make half your plate fruits and vegetables. Choose red, orange, and dark green vegetables like tomatoes, sweet potatoes, and broccoli. The more colorful your plate, the more vitamins, minerals, and fiber your body gets.

- Make half the grains you eat whole grains. Switch to whole-wheat bread instead, and try brown rice, bulgur, buckwheat, oatmeal, quinoa, and wild rice.

- Switch to fat-free or low-fat (1 percent) milk.

- Choose lean protein foods. Meat, poultry, seafood, dry beans or peas, eggs, nuts, and seeds are all protein sources. Switch to leaner cuts of ground beef (labeled 90 percent lean or higher), turkey breast, or chicken breast.

- Cut back on sodium. Choose lower-sodium versions of foods like soup, bread, and frozen meals.

- Drink water instead of sugary drinks.

- Include seafood in your diet. Fish and shellfish have protein, minerals, and healthy fats.

- Cut back on solid fat. Eat fewer foods that contain solid fats like butter, margarine, shortening, and lard. Typical sources include cakes, cookies, and other desserts; pizza; processed and fatty meats; and ice cream.

Exercise: Keeping a Food Journal

If you think your eating habits need improving, but you're not sure where to start, a **food journal** can reveal the patterns that you need to address as you heal from secondary trauma. With a bit of searching, you can find many commercially available food journals available as websites, apps, paper diaries, and other forms. Some even encourage you to take a picture of everything you eat. If you'd like to create your own version from scratch, here's a format you can follow. You can copy it into your secondary trauma notebook, but you may want to use a separate book so the record won't be interrupted by other exercises.

Fill in your food journal as soon as possible after eating. When you can't add the information right away, take a picture of the meal before you begin to eat, to help you capture accurate data. Look for patterns that are revealed from day to day, and set goals to help you improve your patterns.

Week of:	Day:	
Breakfast	Fruits/Veg.	Feelings
Lunch	Fruits/Veg.	Feelings
Dinner	Fruits/Veg.	Feelings
Snacks & Drinks	Fruits/Veg.	Feelings
Daily/Weekly Patterns:		
What I'm working on:		

	Activity:	
	Ate Mindfully? Yes/No	How Full?
	Ate Mindfully? Yes/No	How Full?
	Ate Mindfully? Yes/No	How Full?
	Ate Mindfully? Yes/No	How Full?

Exercise: Mindful Eating

We've mentioned the value of mindfulness in previous chapters (see page 73). Slowing down to eat mindfully will make it easier to observe and describe your experience, so you can update your food diary or just to connect more with your eating habits. Eating more slowly and thoughtfully also helps your appetite stay in sync with your consumption; when we eat quickly, we take in excess calories before our body can tell us we're full. Here are some ways to bring mindfulness to your meals:

Use a timer. Set it to give yourself forty-five seconds to one minute between bites.

Eliminate other distractions. Shut off the television, computer, or phone so you'll notice the sensations of eating. Those signals help your body gauge how much food to consume and when to stop eating.

Put your fork down between bites. Notice what it's like to slow down and pay attention to eating your food. Notice flavors and textures. Notice any emotions that come up, and let them go.

Be curious about the act of eating. Observe yourself while you eat, and ask yourself questions. Write down the answers in your notebook afterward if you like, or just think about these prompts:

- What do you notice about your eating style? Do you eat very fast? Slow? Do you taste your food? Do you enjoy the smells?

- Can you taste the subtle flavors of particular spices in each bite? Do you notice textures?

- As you eat, can you feel layers or levels of fullness in your stomach? Can you rate your fullness by a percentage throughout the meal?

Observe your thinking and feeling. Are your thoughts focused on the activity of eating or on other topics? Do you feel pleasure during the meal? Are you relaxed or rushed? Observe all of your reactions. Don't judge. Be curious.

Your Self-Care Plan

In this chapter, we examined the physical effects that secondary trauma can have on the body. We learned that trauma shifts our brain into survival mode, releasing chemicals that prepare our body to fight, flee, or freeze in reaction to danger. Sometimes our brain has difficulty realizing when we're safe, and our body is harmed by remaining in that trauma-activated state for a prolonged period.

Begin your healing journey by understanding that **the mind and body are connected**. Experience this by using the mind-body awareness exercise on page 89. Exercise is a potent tool for boosting both mental and physical health; consider trying **tai chi** or some other structured, beginner-friendly exercise class. Group exercise will also help you strengthen social connections, which we'll discuss in the next chapter. Use the **yogic breathing exercise** on page 91 to calm your mind and body and manage stress.

Sleep is one of your body's most powerful tools for healing. Practice good **sleep hygiene** and try the **sleep meditation** exercise on page 96. Keep a **dream log** if you're troubled by dreams or nightmares. Try a sleep monitor to assess the quality of your sleep. Discuss significant sleep problems or nightmares with your doctor or therapist.

As you **increase your awareness of your physical symptoms,** use the exercise on page 100 to assess your skill at interpreting your body's messages. Use the chart on page 101 to track the symptoms you're working on. Fill out the wheel of health to prioritize the aspects of your physical health you'd like to improve.

Nourish your body and mind by improving your eating habits. Work on eight basic nutrition goals, and use a food diary to see patterns in the way you eat. Practice mindful eating.

Use the chart on page 51, at the end of chapter 2, to record your self-care plan and stages of change.

Takeaways:

+ The emotional impact of trauma can affect physical health and well-being in many ways.

+ Healing the mind is enhanced by healing the body, and vice versa. Understanding the connection between the mind and body is vital to an overall healing process.

+ Improving our sleep, exercise, and nutrition habits will help us heal.

+ A good sleep hygiene routine is key for enjoying more restful, rejuvenating sleep.

+ Learning to pay attention to the messages your body is sending takes time and practice. Responding to these messages can aid the recovery process.

+ Increasing our awareness of our eating habits is an important step in nourishing the body with good nutrition.

CHAPTER 5

Your Relationships

Throughout this book, we've seen real-life examples of people affected by secondary trauma, and you may have noticed that their stories also affect their families, friends, and coworkers. The mental and physical effects of secondary trauma exposure definitely have an impact on your relationships with other people. In this chapter, we'll discuss how alienation from your social group may play out and how we can even lose touch with who we are. You'll learn some new skills to enhance your self-compassion, evaluate and invigorate your social relationships, and increase social self-care and your connections with others. You may feel that your trauma experience has separated you from people you love and care about. But relationships, even long-neglected ones, can be improved with time and attention—and this includes our relationship with ourselves.

Connection versus Isolation

Isolation is a common experience among people exposed to secondary trauma. You may feel so overwhelmed that it seems easier to avoid other people. You worry about your symptoms being triggered in front of other people, or you don't want to burden anyone with your struggle, or you're certain that no one will understand what you're going through. Isolating yourself enables you to avoid difficult conversations with your spouse, your boss, your children, your friends. Your patience may feel so thin that it's easier to isolate than to try to interact with others.

Connection, in contrast, can be remarkably healing and centering. When you're tempted to cut yourself off from your social group, consider the ways in which connection boosts your well-being:

People are our plumb line. A contractor who's hanging drywall or wallpaper first draws a plumb line, a properly placed guideline to hang the first piece straight. Our social connections provide us with much the same function. They help us see when our emotions, behavior, or physical state are no longer in line with who we really are. They can give us feedback about our actions. And they can be models of behavior that guide us to better functioning.

Connection helps us cope. Very often, other people help us manage our trauma symptoms more effectively than we can on our own. When we're sad, the most effective action we can take is seeking comforting from others. When we're struggling with a problem, running it past a close friend may lead to a quicker solution than trying to do it alone. If we are becoming self-critical, friends can remind us of our successes and our talents.

Self-Alienation

In a case of secondary trauma, the alienation that occurs can often be termed **self-alienation**. When you've experienced trauma, you feel significantly different in the aftermath, and you might conclude that others in your circle don't understand you anymore. So you separate yourself from those around you, feeling like you don't belong. You stop contributing to conversations during meetings and eat alone when you have your lunch. You don't return phone calls or texts. You are alienating yourself from others because you feel like you don't belong.

Trauma can also lead to another type of self-alienation: loss of identity. Exposure to trauma can challenge your sense of who you are, leaving you feeling like a stranger to yourself. You may feel you're not as brave, strong, safe, or competent as you thought you were. This crisis in identity can lead to depression, hopelessness, and low self-esteem.

The solution for self-alienation is to identify the cause and work on increasing connection to yourself and others. It's a concept we'll return to again and again in this chapter: Connection is the antidote to isolation, even if it takes hard work to reconnect.

Exercise: Observing Kindness

One thinking trap many trauma survivors fall into involves beating ourselves up for any mistakes we make or anytime things don't go right. Trauma exposure leaves us looking for ways to prevent future catastrophes, so perhaps we're heaping criticism on ourselves to keep from repeating a mistake. We inflict negative talk on ourselves that we'd never utter to our children, our spouse, or our friends.

The solution is self-compassion: acknowledging our own humanity and that we deserve to be treated with the same care and concern that we offer to others who are hurting.

It takes practice to turn off the negative self-talk that comes with secondary trauma, so use the exercises in chapter 3 to work at muting your inner critic. But you can also draw on your social network for help. Think of the kindest people you know, the ones in your circle whom everyone turns to for advice, who always feel present when you talk to them. Spend time with them and notice how they listen, react, and show caring. When you catch yourself engaging in negative self-talk, replace it with the words your kind friends would say.

Exercise: Active Listening

Good listeners are very valued in society. In Dale Carnegie's famous book *How to Win Friends and Influence People*, he emphasized the importance of listening as a skill for any businessman wanting to become more influential and successful. Secondary trauma affects our ability to be good listeners because listening takes high levels of attention and concentration, capacities that are weakened during trauma recovery.

When you're ready to start reconnecting with your social group, consider it a chance to build up your skills as a good listener. Here's how to be a skillful listener with a friend:

Listen actively. Use eye contact, nodding, and other body language to show your reactions to what you're hearing. Keep comments small and reactive, such as "Oh no!" "I'm so sorry," or "That is awful," to express attention without interrupting the story.

Be a mirror. Reflect what you're hearing back to your friend, so they know how it sounds to a listener. You could say, "You sound sad about your supervisor transferring from your section," or "You seem really concerned you might not like your new supervisor as much as this one." This shows that you're listening deeply but also focusing on them and their problem.

Ask clarifying questions. Use "who, when, what, where, how" questions to move the conversation along and to show interest and concern, and to make sure you understand what's being said.

Don't discount their emotions. Beware of trying to cheer someone up who's having a bad day; sympathize with their feelings instead. Avoid being judgmental. Instead of offering solutions, give the speaker an opportunity to draw conclusions.

GO DEEPER:
Rebuilding Your Relationship with Yourself

Secondary trauma can isolate us from ourselves. But self-introspection is part of being a healthy person. The following is a series of writing prompts that can help you reconnect with yourself and get to know the person you are now.

Write the questions and answers in your notebook. Review your responses anytime you're feeling disconnected from your own identity. Revisit the prompts and write new responses from time to time as you rebuild your relationship with yourself and others.

Describe yourself in detail, as if introducing yourself to someone new for the first time. Outline the major highlights of your life so far, starting in childhood, with enough detail for a good snapshot of the basic structure of your life.

Write about the things you like and dislike: foods, activities, people, any other category you choose. What brings you joy? What makes things unpleasant? How do you decide what you like or dislike?

List three of the biggest challenges you've been through in your life. What have you learned from each? What growth was gained? What did the experiences bring to other aspects of your life?

Write the story of your exposure to trauma. Begin the story before the trauma began, including your general state of mind and self-awareness. Then tell the narrative of your exposure to trauma, including your thoughts and feelings, from beginning to end. Take your time, and if you become overwhelmed, stop writing and return to it another time.

»

« Write about what you were like a month after the trauma, one year after the trauma (if that much time has passed), and now. Write about current struggles and strengths. Explore the ways that you are stronger, more aware, or better than you were before the trauma.

Write as if you're in the future and functioning very well. Describe how you accomplished this better sense of self and how you overcame the trauma symptoms that were causing you the most problems. Write about what your life is like at work and at home now that you're better.

Your Friends and Social Life

Maintaining friendships and a social life takes time and intentional effort. In times of high stress we often think spending time alone will help, but spending time with others tends to help much more. People can help us regulate stress along with helping us normalize experiences and laugh at ourselves. People with good social connections have lower depression and lower stress. And in particular, good social support leads to lower levels of cortisol (see chapter 4), and it seems to quiet biological activity related to stress (Keicolt-Glaser, Gouin, and Hantsoo, 2010). This is all vital when recovering from trauma.

Making new friends and connecting with existing ones may involve stepping outside your comfort zone, if you've been isolating yourself. Here are some ways to build, or rebuild, your social life.

Be a joiner. Try joining a club or group, volunteering, starting a new hobby with friends, taking a class, or inviting coworkers to your home for dinner. See it as an opportunity to try something you've been meaning to do, with the added bonus of meeting people. Ask a friend to take a class with you, so you'll have an excuse to reconnect.

Look for others like you. It's healthy to have a variety of people in your social circle who reflect the different roles in your life. For example, if you're a father, talking with other guys who are raising children will be important. Meeting other people in your profession can help you advance your career and give you a chance to discuss challenges that others wouldn't understand. Talking with another trauma survivor may help you feel less isolated (we'll discuss support groups in chapter 6).

Look for instrumental support. Not every social relationship needs to be a source of emotional sustenance. Instrumental support is any activity that provides practical help or service. You might have a neighbor who's good with home repair and offer babysitting in exchange for fixing your leaky faucet. Maybe you can give a friend a ride to work, and they can pick up some groceries for you when you're too exhausted to go out.

Participate in rituals or traditions that bring you together with friends. It's harder to skip a lunch or bowling night if it's part of your weekly or monthly routine. And if there's a standing appointment to get together, you don't have to make an extra effort to invite people or see who's available.

Be open to spontaneity. If you're feeling social on a particular day, take advantage of it. Make a pot of chili and invite friends over. Call someone you haven't spoken to in a while. Step out to say hello to the neighbor who's passing by.

Healthy Withdrawal versus Isolation

When you're sad, anxious, or under high stress, it's not unusual to want some alone time. You want to escape from stimulation, be in a quiet and calm environment, and have no demands put on you. This is called healthy withdrawal, and it's a good coping skill. The goal of healthy withdrawal is to actively re-center yourself, so you can return to connecting with others.

But when healthy withdrawal morphs into isolation, it's no longer a healthy strategy. The behaviors differ in two important ways:

Duration: Healthy withdrawal may last as little as a half hour and rarely lasts more than a few hours. It will never go on for days at a time.

Activity: Healthy withdrawal is a very intentional, targeted time when we re-center with reading, meditation, exercise, journaling, rest, or any activity that will calm us and prepare us to return to social activity with a healthier mind-set. When we isolate ourselves, we seek to numb or distract ourselves. We tend to turn to obsessively playing video games, spending time with social media, or doing other compulsive activities that don't restore our energy.

Exercise: What Kind of Social Life Do You Want?

Everyone has different social needs, but we all need people in our lives for support, entertainment, growth, and community. In this exercise, you'll explore the type of social life that matches your needs and interests.

Answer the following questions in your notebook:

1. For each of the roles and responsibilities in your life, how many people do you know personally who are in a similar position? Use this list, adding roles that apply to you.

   - Parent. Are your children in school? Grown? Do they have special needs?

   - Spouse or partner. Are you in a relationship? Are you single by choice?

- Family. Do you have any other family obligations, like helping a sibling or aging parents?

- Caretaker. Are you responsible for someone else's care?

- Health issues. Do you have chronic or acute health issues that impact your life? Include your trauma recovery in this category.

- Pet owner. Do you live with an animal that you take care of every day?

- Religious or spiritual interest. Do you identify with an organized religion? Do you have spiritual beliefs? Are you an atheist or agnostic?

- Hobbies, interests, and passions. Do you play a musical instrument? Do you play an organized sport or game (anything from chess to poker)? Do you have a love for art or spend time crafting or making things?

- Student. Are you in school or pursuing an advanced degree, license, or specialization?

- Add other roles that are part of your life.

2. How many people do you like to socialize with? Rate your preference for each of these activities on a scale from 1 (dislike) to 5 (enjoy very much).

- Large group activities (more than ten people)

- Small group activities (five to ten other people)

- Activities with a few others (two to three other people)

- One-on-one activities

- Activity-based interactions (taking a class, volunteering, exercising, seeing a movie or play)

- Unstructured interactions (meeting for coffee or dinner, going to the park, chatting in the lobby of your apartment building)

3. How much time do you prefer to spend with other people? Ideally, how many hours a week would you want to spend socializing? How often on weekdays, and how often during the weekend (or when you have the day off from work)? How many hours would you prefer to spend at any social interaction?

Review your answers, and write down some examples of what your ideal social life would look like.

If you're just starting to reconnect after a long period of isolation, try planning social events that fall within your preferences. That might mean a short coffee break once a week with one friend, or joining a book club that meets once a month. Initially, try to socialize with people in at least three different roles that you listed. As your social life expands, start looking for new connections to match the other roles on your list.

If you're coping with trauma, avoiding people can make you feel more comfortable at first. But constant avoidance leads to isolation and lack of social support. So it's necessary to practice the opposite behavior: approach people. For this exercise, you'll create a **socialization plan** that consists of ten steps, each gradually increasing your comfort level with social interaction.

Begin with activities that feel low in risk to you, like texting friends, making a social media connection, or calling someone on the phone to catch up.

Move on to medium-risk activities, like face-to-face conversations over coffee, seeing a movie with one or more friends, or taking a walk with work colleagues during a break.

For the final steps, consider events that you'd like to participate in but seemed out of reach at the start, like attending a sporting event or concert, going to a large party, or joining a hobby group.

Copy the following chart into your notebook, filling in the steps with activities of your choosing. Or use the example actions if they feel right to you. Remember that each step should be slightly more difficult for you than the previous one and bring you just a bit past your comfort zone. Avoid setting yourself up to make a giant leap. Try each interaction in a time frame that you're comfortable with, working slowly through the list. Repeat each step as often as you need to, and move to the next when you're ready.

Socialization Plan

Steps	Action	Time Frame	Completed
1	Text three people per day to check in.	3 weeks	
2	Say hello to two different coworkers daily. Smile.	2 weeks	
3	Make one phone call per day and talk at least 5 minutes.	2 weeks	
4	Go out to lunch with someone weekly.	1 month	
5	Start a conversation with someone new daily.	2 weeks	
6	Say yes: Attend a social event you are invited to.	2 months	
7	Invite someone to go to the movies or another event with you weekly.	1 month	
8	Say yes: Agree to go to a social event you would usually refuse.	4 total events	
9	Invite a group of people over for a social activity.	2 total events	
10	Participate in a social activity and talk to three people less familiar.	2 total events	

Exercise: Rate the Difficulty of Alternative Behaviors

In this exercise, you'll decide which social behaviors to work on by assessing how difficult they are. You can then choose to start with the least difficult behaviors, to give yourself some successes. Or, if you feel up to it, you might dive into a medium-difficulty challenge that seems rewarding. You can also use the results of this evaluation to fill in your socialization plan (previous exercise).

Copy the following chart, rating each of the behaviors listed from 1 (never) to 5 (always). For any behavior you rate as "rarely" or "never," consider a socialization plan that will ease you into it. If you prefer, you can replace the example behaviors with similar ones that are more relevant to you.

	Behavior	Rating (1-5)	Plan
1	I feel comfortable in restaurants.	2	Meet friend for lunch at a place I'm familiar with.
2	My social circle meets my needs for connection.	2	Join friends at the dog park on Saturdays.
3	I enjoy attending sporting events.		
4	I look forward to a party at a friend's house.		
5	I enjoy checking in with family when I get home from work.		
6	I use my alone time very wisely.		Set up an area in my house to do yoga stretches on my day off.

	Behavior	Rating (1-5)	Plan
7	I have a healthy relationship with video games or other screen time.		
8	I regularly connect with my friends.		
9	My spouse or partner and I enjoy regular dates.		
10	I am happy to help my family with problems.		
11	I have healthy work friendships.		
12	I utilize my relationships for help emotionally.		
13	My friends turn to me for help.		
14	My relationships tend to energize me.		
15	I have a healthy relationship with myself.		

Exercise: Your Plan for Change

Now that you've been considering which aspects of improving your social connection are more challenging, this exercise will help you focus on the areas you'd like to improve. Copy the following chart into your notebook, and choose three challenging areas relating to your social relationships. For each one, identify the resources (people, skills, knowledge, or behaviors) that will help you do better. Then list any missing emotional or practical skills that you'll need to accomplish your plan. Finally, describe a plan to tackle the challenge, using the resources you listed and the techniques you've read about in this book.

My Plan for Change

Area of Challenge	Area of Challenge	Area of Challenge
Turning to friends for emotional support	Checking in with family when I get home	Poor relationship with video games
Resources	Resources	Resources
Good friends, my spouse, good communication skills	My kids, and spouse's willingness	My spouse, my friends
Missing Skills	Missing Skills	Missing Skills
Identifying feelings, self-accountability	A protocol for check-in, patience	Time management, self-control
Plan	Plan	Plan
Talk to three friends weekly and share my feelings about work and my current symptoms	Talk to two friends about how they check in, set a time to check in	Lock up game console, make list of alternative activities that are healthier

Your Work Life

If you're working a job that exposes you to trauma, and you choose to remain in that field, changing your relationship with your work life is an important part of your recovery. And if your trauma isn't related to your work, a healthy relationship with your job is still important for reducing stress and helping you heal.

The best way to address this is to make sure you have a good **work-life balance**. This means allowing enough time and energy to take care of yourself so that you can be at your best both at work and outside of work. Here are some principles to follow:

Create boundaries between your work and your life. If you think about work a lot when you're not there, if you talk more about work than any other topic, if you identify yourself by your job title more than any other role (parent, spouse, sibling, friend) or passion (runner, painter, chess player, antique collector), you need to establish practices that keep your job from spilling into other areas of your life. Leave the work talk at work. Don't bring paperwork or other materials home unless absolutely necessary. Socialize with friends who have different jobs than yours. Cultivate interests and hobbies that aren't related to your work.

Make a transition plan. If you arrive home from work feeling tired, drained, and irritable, a routine that everyone can follow may help you transition from work life to home life. For example, you may find it helpful to have some alone time so you can change clothes and let go of the day's concerns. You might want to say hello to everyone one-on-one instead of all at once. Or you might go for a short walk after a difficult day, or play catch with the kids, to burn off some tension. Discuss the issue with your family and come up with a routine that everyone is aware of and agrees to.

Create a better relationship with your workplace. Take time to remind yourself why your job is meaningful and why you decided to enter this field. Maintain friendly relations and camaraderie with the people you work with.

Determine a process for regular growth in your job. Think about a promotion you'd like, or a different position, and find out what you need to do to get it. Pursue additional training and specialization when it's available. Find a mentor who will help you navigate your career path.

Remind yourself how your occupation fits into your future plans and goals. Are you saving for a home or a vacation? Are you gaining experience to set up a private practice? Track your progress toward your goal. When you reach a work-related milestone, like a promotion, hiring anniversary, or certification, give yourself a reward. Take the time to do something fun to acknowledge your hard work.

Notice what you and your coworkers are doing right. It can be easy to allow negativity to leak into your attitude and thinking, especially in a high-pressure job that exposes you to trauma. Fight this tendency. Comment on your successes, and be generous with praising your colleagues. Thank people when they help you, and don't let anyone's hard work go unnoticed.

Make sure you take breaks. If you tend to work through lunch, even when you don't have to, consider changing this strategy and using the time to clear your mind. If breaks are impossible on some days, get up and walk around, even for a minute, to stretch your muscles and catch your breath.

Stay organized. If you're not a naturally organized person, work on those skills. Get help and advice from others who have very good organizational processes (every workplace has at least one such person). Being organized can reduce your stress, eliminating distractions so you can focus on important tasks.

Watch for compassion fatigue. Professions that expose you to secondary trauma can be a strain on your capacity for compassion. Read about compassion fatigue in chapter 2.

Track how you are coping with ongoing stress and trauma related to your work. Use the exercises in this book to remain aware of how stress is affecting you and to reduce that stress by managing your emotions, thoughts, physical symptoms, and social relationships.

Oscar's Story

Oscar has been working for a large police agency for fourteen years. He's responded to his share of difficult calls but thought he was coping with his job stress fairly well. Recently Oscar's wife, Karen, told him she was considering filing for divorce. She was tired of his moodiness, his lack of communication, and his refusal to go out socially with her. Oscar was shocked. He thought they were doing fine; he always apologized to her after he lashed out, and he never got upset if she went out by herself. Her ultimatum opened his eyes, and Oscar realized he needed to work on their relationship. He agreed that they should go to couples' therapy.

The therapist conducted a thorough assessment and found that Oscar had post-traumatic stress disorder (PTSD, a medical diagnosis that covers the symptoms discussed in this book). Oscar was confused because he'd never been in a shooting. The therapist explained how secondary trauma can lead to PTSD and how it tends to impact relationships. She asked Karen a series of questions about his behavior, early in their relationship and more recently. Oscar listened intently as his wife painted a picture of him becoming more and more socially isolated, his growing irritability and short fuse, his avoidance of his family by playing video games for hours at a time, and even his thrashing around at night when he had nightmares.

The therapist referred Oscar to an individual therapist so he could work specifically on his trauma. Oscar and his wife continued to work on their relationship. He learned to find better ways to deal with his emotions, he built up neglected friendships, and he worked on getting better sleep. He gave up video games altogether for a time in an effort to break the habit of using them to numb and isolate himself. Meanwhile, Karen had to confront her habit of walking on eggshells and not communicating her concerns, and her avoidance of Oscar when he seemed to be having a bad day. They slowly began to realize that they'd both adjusted to Oscar's trauma in unhealthy ways.

Oscar knew he had a long way to go, but he felt hope and resolve now that he knew there were skills he could learn. His relationship with Karen began to feel close again, he was feeling happier, his friendships were flourishing, and he noticed he was enjoying his job. Oscar and Karen began to talk about working with their children next, to break any unhealthy patterns they'd adopted in response to Oscar's trauma. Oscar loved the idea of collaborating with his wife and creating a stronger home environment. He felt like himself for the first time in years.

What Are Your Most Important Work Relationships?

One of the most recent extensive Gallup polls (2019) found that workers are happier and more engaged when they have a good relationship with an engaged boss, when they receive praise, when they feel encouraged and cared about, and when they have friendships at work. We spend so many hours at our jobs, it's clear that our lives are much better when we're happier at work.

Good relations with your workmates can boost your happiness while on the job and help you be more social. For this exercise, make a list in your notebook of the people you frequently interact with in your workplace, using the following chart. Rate your relationship with each person as excellent, good, fair, or poor. (Don't overthink it; your gut assessment is probably accurate.) Note any factors that may be contributing to the relationship.

Next, choose one person whose standing is rated at fair or poor, who you'd most like to have a better relation with. Review the activity list on page 124 and formulate a plan to strengthen that relationship. Write the details in your notebook. Implement your plan, and reevaluate the relationship after several weeks. If it's improved, move on to the next person on your list.

Review the entire list periodically, to make sure you're maintaining positive connections with your workmates.

Name	Original rating	Notes	Improvement plan	New rating
Blair	Excellent	We always cover for each other.		
Doug	Good	Helped him when his computer crashed.		
Tim O.	Poor	Don't know him very well. We disagreed about a meeting schedule.	Compliment the last presentation he gave. Ask for advice about current workload.	

Here are some actions that can improve workplace relationships:

Provide some small help to a particular workmate every day for a couple of weeks. Don't do it for attention; do it from generosity. Do not worry about reciprocity.

Encourage a coworker whom you know is particularly burdened with a work task. Let them know you've noticed their hard work and that you're impressed with their tenacity.

Let your supervisor know when you see them being a good leader. Respond to an e-mail with specific, sincere praise. Thank them briefly when you run into them in the hall.

Take opportunities to work with different coworkers. Make it a goal to cooperate with someone that you might have a hard time working with. Consider taking a more subservient role on a project and allowing your colleague to take the lead.

Get to know some things about your coworkers' personal lives. You don't have to force a friendship, but ask how a coworker's child is doing on their soccer team. Ask about a supervisor's vacation. Comment on someone's new car. Always show your interest in their happiness.

Seek help from a supervisor or coworker regarding a subject you know they're particularly skilled in. Ask insightful questions about a process you want to learn more about. Let them know how grateful you are for their generosity in helping you understand.

Exercise: How Has Trauma Impacted Your Close Relationships?

At the same time we're changing our behavior due to trauma, our loved ones are making their own adjustments to cope with our new behaviors. They may not notice their own changes even as we don't always notice ours. But the cumulative effects of hundreds of small adjustments can add up to significant dysfunction. As you continue with your healing process, it's important that you learn how family and friends have adjusted to your trauma, so you can repair and reconnect those relationships.

For this exercise, ask three or four family members or close friends to meet with you separately for a structured interview. Explain that you want to understand how your trauma has affected them, and it would help you if they'd answer some questions so you can learn some ways to begin strengthening the relationship.

For the interview, use some or all of the following questions. You can add your own. You can record the questions and answers in your notebook or, with the interviewee's permission, record the interview with your phone or device.

- Do you think I am more irritable or aggressive than I was five years ago (or pick a time frame from before your trauma exposure)? What does that look like to you? What am I doing, saying, or acting like when I'm aggressive?

- Have you noticed a change in my ability to concentrate? What does that look like to you? Give me some examples.

- Do I seem to be more negative than I used to be? What are some things I do or say, if this is the case?

- Do you feel I have a normal range of emotions, positive and negative? What do you notice about this?

- Do you feel as connected to me as you used to? What's different about how I interact with you?

- Do I get as excited about activities or family time as I used to? What's different about how I am now?

- Do you feel I'm different to communicate with than I used to be? What do you notice has changed?

- Do you feel that I can relax like I used to? What's different?

- When I get upset, do you feel I cope with it in healthy ways? What can you tell me about this?

- Do I spend too much time zoning out or numbing myself? What can you tell me about this?

- Do you feel we're as social with each other as we used to be? What's different?

- Share with me any other differences you notice that you feel would be good for me to know.

Take notes while you conduct the interview, and compare people's answers. Patterns or similar answers among different interviews suggest areas where your trauma symptoms have most impacted your relationships.

Exercise: Loving-Kindness Meditation for Work

If you've come this far, you've worked hard. This meditative exercise expresses your desire for recovery and will help foster compassion for yourself and those you work with. Research on this type of meditation, known as a "loving-kindness meditation," shows that its practice can increase positive feelings and self-acceptance, create more resilience, reduce pain, and enhance social connectedness (Aspy and Proeve, 2017). Feel free to adapt the language to include anyone you'd like to feel connected with.

Start by relaxing into a comfortable position, sitting or lying down. Breathe deeply. Let your mind slow down, and allow your body to become relaxed. Say each of the following statements to yourself, slowly, out loud if you can. (Once you've learned the text well enough to recite it from memory, you can close your eyes during the meditation.) Feel the emotional meaning of each statement.

May I be happy in every area of my life.

May I be strong enough to overcome my struggles.

May I be safe and remember my training.

May I be healthy in mind and body.

May I be at peace with my choices.

Next, bring to mind someone in your workplace whom you feel close to, admire, or feel helpful toward. While keeping this person in your mind, say these statements with meaning:

May they be happy in every area of their life.

May they be strong enough to overcome their struggles.

May they be safe and remember their training.

May they be healthy in mind and body.

May they be at peace with their choices.

Finally, bring to mind a sense of the collective body of people who serve in your workplace or your field in general. While keeping them in your mind, say these statements with meaning:

May we all be happy in every area of our lives.

May we be strong enough to overcome our struggles.

May we be safe and remember our training.

May we be healthy in mind and body.

May we be at peace with our choices.

Practice this loving-kindness meditation daily.

Your Self-Care Plan

In this chapter we saw that overcoming social isolation, self-alienation, and the ways that trauma impacts your relationships will provide you with an increased sense of happiness and life satisfaction. The social self-care described in this chapter will be somewhat different to implement, compared to some of the more internal goals we discussed in previous chapters. Things become more complicated when other people are involved, after all.

Attending to social relationships that have been affected by secondary trauma starts with understanding why **isolation is a common but unhealthy response to a traumatic experience**. Trauma can make it difficult to be with other people, but we need our social network to help us heal. **Connection** is the only cure for isolation.

It's also important to know that we **sometimes become isolated from ourselves,** because trauma can challenge our sense of self. **Self-compassion** is critical for reconnecting to who we are. The exercises in chapter 3 can help counter negative thoughts and self-talk that inhibit self-compassion. **Observing kindness in others**, page 115, can give us a model for being kinder to ourselves.

To begin reconnecting with friends and family, use the **listening skills** described on page 116.

For deeper work in rebuilding your connection to yourself, use the **writing prompts** on page 117.

Use the tactics on page 120 to rebuild a neglected social life.

Know the difference between **healthy withdrawal** and self-isolation.

Try the **values worksheet** on pages 46–47 to help you focus on the kind of social life that you want, and create a **socialization plan** to ease you toward your goals. Use the worksheet on page 127 to zero in on the social behaviors that you find most difficult, and make a plan for change to address those challenging activities.

Make sure you have a **healthy work-life balance**, especially if your career exposes you to trauma.

Value the connections you make with the people you work with. **Rate your workplace relationships**, and try to improve the ones that are poor.

Ask friends and family members to share their observations about the impact your struggle with secondary trauma has had on them. Use the **structured interview questions** on pages 134–135.

Improve your compassion for yourself and others with the **loving-kindness meditation** beginning on page 135.

Use the chart on page 51, at the end of chapter 2, to record your self-care plan and stages of change.

Takeaways:

+ Isolation may feel easier in the short term, but it has long-term consequences. Building connections can aid healing from trauma.

+ Learning to extend the same compassion to yourself that you do to others will give you a better emotional environment for your journey.

+ Building or rebuilding your relationships with family and friends is possible. A robust social life looks different to different people, but the results are the same for everyone: increased health and happiness.

+ Avoidance can become a habit in the aftermath of trauma. Overcoming these patterns is best addressed directly and systematically.

+ Work is a necessary part of our lives. Learning to maximize work satisfaction while minimizing work stress should be an ongoing process involving regular evaluation and goal setting.

CHAPTER 6
The Road Ahead

This book is a recovery guide, and like any guidebook it's not meant to be read once and then put on a shelf. It's a reference tool that you should use whenever you need it. Or think of it as a road map—a resource that you may not require when you're in familiar territory, but it's handy to have when you take a wrong turn or find yourself detoured.

Recovery from trauma is a journey toward remission, a state in which your symptoms are at such a low level that they're readily manageable and not significantly impacting your day-to-day life. Technically speaking, even when you're feeling healed and haven't experienced any disturbing trauma symptoms for a long time, we don't use the term *cured*. It's always possible that high stress levels or overexposure to further trauma might cause some symptoms to resurface. But don't let that worry you. Rely on the self-care techniques you've learned, and when the going gets rough, take extra care of yourself to remain resilient in the face of stress and trauma exposure. Self-care is the medicine that counteracts trauma, and you're in control of administering it.

This chapter will help you establish the mind-set you'll need to maintain your recovery over the long term. You'll learn to document your victories and celebrate your progress, you'll understand the challenges you've faced and the ones to come, and you'll commit to building on your successes and continuing your journey of recovery.

Long-Term Outlook

Working through the results of trauma is a lifelong process. Once you reach a state of remission, it's important to keep to a level of self-care that allows you to function at your best. Keep these principles in mind as you bring your symptoms under control, and review them periodically to maintain the wellness that you worked so hard to achieve:

Keep aware of your triggers and symptoms. No one knows you as well as you know yourself, so it's important that you remain aware of the triggers you identified in chapter 2 and that you're alert for any reemergence of trauma symptoms. Many trauma survivors experience symptoms to some degree even when in remission. But usually they're mild and easy to deal with. If you suspect a new trigger is affecting you, or symptoms are becoming more intense or frequent than usual, refer to the appropriate chapters in this book to identify, track, and manage the situation. And always increase your self-care when feeling stressed or exposed to trauma, as a preventive measure.

Watch for habit creep. As we've seen, the habits that we form in the aftermath of trauma can be unhealthy. You've worked hard to replace them with healthier, sustainable behaviors. But that doesn't mean the old habits are gone forever. Be alert for old, bad habits that creep back into your life, like isolation and avoidance, negative thinking, and poor behavior relating to nutrition, sleep, and exercise. Examine the emotions that feed these habits (chapter 2) and the thoughts that prompt them (chapter 3). Check in with family and friends to see if they've noticed a change in your behavior, and accept their feedback. We'll talk more about building good habits later in this chapter.

Make self-care a priority. You've heard this before, but it bears repeating: Self-care is the foundation of your recovery. Self-care is not selfish; it's actually selfless. When you're healthy, you are the best version of yourself. And that allows you to be there more effectively for your family, friends, and work responsibilities. Imagine all your stress on one side of a scale and all your self-care on the other. The amount of care you're giving to yourself should more than outweigh the stress, so the scale stays tilted in your favor if something unexpected adds to your stress level.

Notice and celebrate your post-traumatic growth. Many people who enter remission after trauma find that the experience has granted some additional strengths and insights. One group of researchers at the University of North Carolina at Charlotte identified five different ways that one can show resilience after trauma: seeing yourself as more resilient and tougher than before the trauma; experiencing a deepening of your personal relationships; recognizing more meaning in your life; being more grateful; and seeing new opportunities that you hadn't noticed before (Tedeschi, Shakespeare-Finch, Taku, and Calhoun, 2018).

Expect change. The growth you experience may include a change in what you consider to be meaningful in your life. This isn't unusual after recovery from trauma. Things that were important to you before may seem less significant now. You may find a new focus, devoting yourself to a cause, mentoring coworkers, or even changing careers. Your recovery may leave you much more thankful for small things that you hadn't paid attention to in the past. New feelings of gratitude can bring you a deep happiness you didn't have before. And with your trauma symptoms quieter, you'll likely feel more capable and content in various aspects of your life.

Remember the work you've done. This is especially important if you continue in the career or circumstances that exposed you to secondary trauma. Keep this book and your notebook accessible, and take time to review what you learned about yourself.

Exercise: Your Biggest Victories So Far

If we don't recognize the importance of the changes we make, we won't sustain them. In this exercise, you'll document and celebrate what you've learned during your recovery. Take the opportunity to be proud of what you accomplished. Acknowledge your struggle, and feel the deep satisfaction of overcoming so many obstacles.

Use the following list to record your successes in your notebook. Think carefully to explore what you've learned about each aspect of your recovery. Return to the list anytime you need motivation, and add to it as your recovery progresses.

List at least five successes for each of these categories:

- Symptoms I'm aware of

- Symptoms that have improved

- Feelings I have worked on

- Feelings I am more comfortable with

- Thinking patterns I have worked on

- Ways I know my thinking has improved

- Action/behavior patterns I have worked on

- Areas of my physical health I have worked on

- Ways my physical health has improved

- New self-care I have worked on

- Relationships I have worked on

- Ways I have improved relationships

- Areas of my work I have worked on

- Areas of my work that have improved

- Evidence that I'm more resilient

Your Biggest Challenges So Far

This exercise will help you explore your relationships with your biggest challenges. Copy the following chart into your notebook, and fill in the details for up to four different challenges that you've faced. Try to touch on different categories of trauma symptoms: emotional, thought-based, physical, relationship-based. Recall how the challenge felt when you first approached it (check back in your notebook), where the challenge stands now, and what it would be like for you if the symptoms were completely eliminated.

Area of Challenge: *Anger*

What It Looked Like at Its Worst: *Daily "fits," family walking on eggshells, getting in trouble at work*

What It Looks Like Now: *Less than weekly "fits," not as strong and don't last long, catch myself effectively most of the time, family is relaxing, no trouble at work*

What It Would Look Like Repaired: *Not feeling any anger at all*

Is This Realistic?: *No, anger won't go away*

My Next Step: *Learning to accept anger as an emotion, recognizing I can feel it without acting out on it*

The Road to Progress Isn't Always Straight

Noticing your symptoms—their duration, intensity, and frequency—is vital to your recovery. Should any well-managed symptoms become more difficult to handle, don't consider this a setback. Recurring symptoms are more like a bend in the road to remission. You can navigate the change as long as you're aware of it. Here are some guidelines to remember:

It helps to touch base. Consider incorporating a regular check-in with your support network to determine the level of your current symptoms. Ask family and friends how they see your symptoms. Discuss specific symptoms like anger or avoidance, asking questions like, "What do you notice about my anger (or any other symptom)? Do you think I'm improving? Give me an example." Tell them the most critical areas that you want them to pay attention to: a particular mood or behavior. Give them permission to share feedback with you when they're concerned.

Prevent symptom recurrence with self-care. Anytime you experience more trauma or heavy stress, watch yourself closely, and devote yourself to your sleep hygiene routine, exercise, meditation, nutrition, support system, and other healthy practices that improve your mood and well-being. Take time off from work, and decrease overtime hours. Schedule pleasant activities that rejuvenate you. Consider establishing a relationship with a therapist who specializes in trauma to gain additional skills and insights, and to obtain additional support.

New symptoms may appear. It's possible that new trauma or acute stress may generate symptoms you haven't experienced before. Apply the tools in chapter 1 anytime you think this may be the case.

New bad habits might substitute for old ones. Be vigilant against replacing bad behaviors with different, but also unhealthy, habits. Consider a caretaker at a veterans care home who used to play video games for hours as a form of avoidance and numbing. As he learned to manage his symptoms and move toward recovery, he gave up the gaming and replaced it with a new routine of social interactions and exercise. This practice remained in place for a few years, until a time of higher stress. He reached out to a friend, and they met at a bar for a beer and a chat. The interaction was helpful, but the caretaker found himself hitting the bar after work for a quick drink, which grew to two drinks, then eventually to drinking daily. The alcohol became a new way to numb himself and added to his problems at home and work in new, complicated ways. Pay attention to your behavior during times of stress or trauma, to make sure you're making healthy choices.

Building Your New Habits

The brain loves habits. They're a sort of automatic algorithm, a way for us to perform familiar actions using less brainpower. According to habit experts, developing a habit successfully involves a few important steps.

First, we determine what action we want to incorporate into our lives. This needs to be something specific enough that we can track and measure the accomplishment. "Exercise more" is too vague. "Go to the gym twice a week" or "Take the stairs instead of the elevator" stand a better chance of becoming habits.

Second, we set up cues or triggers for the habit. These are signals that remind us to engage in the desired activity. Cues are best when they're closely related to the habit: an alarm that goes off at a time when we can exercise, the gym bag that we keep by the front door, a standing meeting with a friend to go for an afternoon walk. The more cues you use, the stronger the habit becomes.

The third component of a good habit is a reward. Provide yourself with an incentive, especially when starting out. Good rewards don't sabotage the overall goal. Treating yourself to dessert after going to the gym will undermine your purpose. But buying a better gym bag after three workouts could be motivating.

When trying to build a healthy habit, make it SMART:

Specific: The goal or habit established needs to be specific enough so that you know you're doing it. "Become closer to my family" sounds good, but how will you tell that you succeeded? Instead, aim to ask each family member about their day.

Measurable: Tracking your progress is key. In the previous example, you might decide to ask three rich questions every work- or school day. This would be a five-day-a-week goal, with three questions for each family member.

Attainable: Remember the woman who wanted to walk two miles a day in chapter 2? Reducing that goal to a quarter mile made much more sense. Be sure your new habit isn't so ambitious that it feels overwhelming.

Relevant: If a goal has no deep meaning for you, you will be unlikely to stick to the habit very long. If needed, take time to write down why you're pursuing the new habit, and review your notes when you're tempted to quit.

Time-bound: A good goal needs to have a time line of some sort. Give yourself enough time to keep the habit from being stressful, but set a deadline that will create some pressure to meet it. You can always try again if the clock runs out.

SMART Goal Setting

This exercise is a more formal approach to building a habit. Guided by the SMART approach, copy the chart into your notebook, and fill in the details to reach your goal. As a rule of thumb, if you want to establish a daily habit, two to three weeks is usually enough time for success. A weekly habit may take a few months to become ingrained.

Specific Goal	Exercise 5 days a week; 20 minutes or more
Method for Measuring or Tracking	Track in exercise book
Resources Needed	Exercise book; athletic shoes; gym membership
What Cues Can I Set Up?	In the morning on the way to work, leave gym bag near back door; set alarm half hour earlier
How Long Will It Take to Achieve	Lifelong, but habit will take about a month to establish
Extrinsic Reward: Temporary Motivation	Coffee at my favorite shop on the way to work after the gym
Intrinsic Reward: What Makes This Meaningful?	I will feel better about myself; I will sleep better; I will be stronger

Watch Out for Red Flags

We all have times in our lives when we struggle more than usual. When you have a history of trauma, it's especially important to understand red flag situations, to intervene with self-care. You can handle red flags if you:

Know your stress range. Each of us has a range for stress that we can function under and a limit beyond which our normal performance begins to break down. Attend to your self-care to keep away from the top end of your range high. Be honest with yourself about how much stress you can tolerate.

Have a plan for emergencies. Sometimes stress becomes out of control because of a sudden crisis or tragedy, like the death of a family member. Circumstances like these may limit your ability to exercise, eat healthy foods, maintain sleep hygiene, spend time with your social circle, and otherwise keep your self-care going strong. Set a deadline for yourself to return to your normal practices as soon as you can. It may help to resume your self-care strategies one at a time, so you're not overwhelmed.

Reprioritize unhealthy relationships. Some people in our lives bring out the best in us, and others . . . not so much. If you're spending significant time with someone who drags down your mood, causes undue stress, or takes up so much time that you neglect other aspects of your life, distance yourself from that detrimental connection. Instead, spend more time with people who lift you up and regenerate you.

Find What Works for You

Recovery from secondary trauma can look entirely different for different people. As you continue your journey into remission, these guiding principles will help you determine which practices to maintain:

Tracking your recovery plan is essential. Determine a tracking strategy that works for you; refer back to earlier exercises to find a format that you like. Use a notebook or digital device to capture thoughts, ideas, or observations about your recovery on the fly. Check in regularly with your support network. Schedule a meeting with yourself, weekly at first, to review your tracking data and plan what's next.

Try new strategies from time to time to renew your enthusiasm for recovery and develop a wider repertoire of self-care. Explore new forms of exercise or new ways to cook healthy meals, try devices and rituals to help with sleep hygiene, plan new social events, learn new meditations and mindfulness practices, or buy a new notebook or app to record your recovery exercises. Go back to exercises and worksheets in this book that you weren't up to trying before. Return to an exercise that you haven't performed for a long time.

Know your Achilles heel. In Greek mythology, the warrior Achilles was invulnerable to all harm . . . except for a spot on his heel, and that was his downfall. Every trauma survivor needs to identify their vulnerabilities—the symptom that strikes hardest, the unhealthy behavior that's easiest to fall back into. You may be excessively vulnerable to lack of sleep and need to spend extra effort on your sleep hygiene. You may be badly triggered by crowds. You may notice that if you don't exercise, you become particularly anxious. Even when your trauma symptoms are well controlled, pay special attention to your most vulnerable spots.

Building Your Support Network

Good social support helps us through the difficulties in our lives and makes them more manageable. Having people in our lives to celebrate the triumphs is also vital, because we want people to see what we look like when we are doing very well.

As you build on your recovery from secondary trauma, review chapter 5 to make sure you **stay connected to your social group**. Once you've reconnected with family and friends and fostered good relationships in your workplace, develop socialization plans (page 124) to widen your social network and make it more diverse. Friends, coworkers, extended family, and neighbors can all contribute different things to your life.

A **trauma support group** can bring a different type of social connection, one that's especially useful if you feel a need to communicate with others who are recovering from trauma. Your doctor or therapist may be able to refer you to an appropriate group. The structure, meeting schedule, fees or donations, and other elements of a support group vary widely. Your best bet is to observe a meeting, avoid groups that seem negative or chaotic, and otherwise attend a few consecutive meetings to see if you feel better. If you do, chances are you've found a good group.

For many, **therapy may be necessary** to address the more difficult aspects of trauma. Finding a good therapist in your community may take time. Ask friends and coworkers for suggestions. Call your insurance company for a list of providers. Many workplaces have employee assistance programs (EAPs) that may be able to give you a list of clinicians in your area. And if you see a therapist and the two of you don't click, don't give up! Therapy works best when there is a good connection between the therapist and yourself. Try again and again until you find the match you need.

Final Thoughts

How do I know the advice in this book works? I've lived it. I have pulled myself up from being actively symptomatic, and I learned to change my self-care to keep myself in remission for years.

Then I again experienced secondary trauma on October 1, 2017. One of my children was shot in the shoulder while attending the Route 91 concert in Las Vegas, where a mass shooting took place. Law enforcement contacts updated me with unfolding details of the event; I heard the screams and gunshots when my daughter called to tell me she was running from the scene. I knew what to do in the aftermath. I talked to my support network and let them know how I was doing. I slept at least eight hours a night. I made sure I was eating well. I wrote down my thoughts. I paid close attention to my thinking. At night I watched stand-up comedians on YouTube until I laughed, then I would go to sleep. After about three months, I reduced my working hours and began to reconstruct the other parts of my life: exercise, active social interaction, and home projects.

I look back on that experience and feel grateful that I was able to manage my trauma recovery. You can start this same journey, and as you move forward you'll find yourself healthier, happier, renewed at work, and able to help others in ways that feel genuinely congruent with your best self.

RESOURCES

For first responders and their families:

Blue H.E.L.P.
Honors police officers, retired or active, who have died
by suicide.
www.bluehelp.org

The Wounded Blue
Assists disabled and injured law enforcement officers by provid-
ing education to departments and individuals to build resiliency
and increase overall wellness.
www.thewoundedblue.org

TEND Academy
Resources and training for first responders and their families.
www.tendacademy.ca

The National Child Traumatic Stress Network
Provides training and resources for therapists working with
abused children.
www.nctsn.org

Safe Call Now
Service for all first responders to help those who are struggling. Safe Call has a 24-hour hotline first responders can call
for support.
www.safecallnow.org

The Code Green Campaign
Educates and destigmatizes mental health issues that impact
first responders.
www.codegreencampaign.org

First Responders' Bridge
Helps first responders and their caregivers get connected to help for trauma.
www.firstrespondersbridge.org

My favorite apps for use with PTSD:

Tactical Breather & Breathe2Relax
Helps people calm and center through intentional breathing.

Provider Resilience
For therapists to track their symptoms of compassion fatigue, burnout, and secondary trauma.

Mindfulness app
Various mindfulness exercises to help you develop these skills.

PTSD Coach
For veterans to track PTSD symptoms and create a resource library to use when symptomatic.

Life Armor
Tools and assessments to examine your relationship with dozens of issues, including anger, depression, resilience, and stress.

For anyone who wants to learn more about secondary trauma:

Ruderman Family Foundation
Conducts research on a variety of topics regarding disabilities. They have published a useful white paper regarding first responder wellness, trauma, PTSD, and suicide.
www.rudermanfoundation.org

National Institute of Mental Health
Provides research, education, and consumer information about mental health issues.
www.nimh.nih.gov

National Alliance on Mental Illness
Offers education and support for those dealing with mental health issues, along with family support through local chapters.
www.nami.org

National Suicide Prevention Lifeline
Provides 24/7 support for anyone having suicidal thoughts. They also provide information for professionals that are considered best practices for suicide response.
www.suicidepreventionlifeline.org

The Vicarious Trauma Toolkit
Information for anyone who wants to learn more about secondary trauma.
vtt.ovc.ojp.gov/what-is-vicarious-trauma

The Body Keeps the Score: Brain, Mind, and Body in the Healing of Trauma.
Van Der Kolk, B. (2014). New York, NY: Penguin Books.
One of the best books describing the ways PTSD manifests in the body.

Why We Sleep: Unlocking the Power of Sleep and Dreams.
Walker, M. (2017). New York, NY: Scribner Press.
The best book about sleep I have ever read. If sleep is your Achilles heel, this book can help enormously.

REFERENCES

American Psychiatric Association. 2013. *Diagnostic and Statistical Manual of Mental Disorders* (5th ed.). Washington, DC: American Psychiatric Publishing.

Arnold, D., L. G. Calhoun, R. Tedeschi, and A. Cann. 2005. "Vicarious Posttraumatic Growth in Psychotherapy." *Journal of Humanistic Psychology* 45, no. 2 (April 1): 239–63.

Aspy, D. J., and M. Proeve. 2017. "Mindfulness and Loving-Kindness Meditation: Effects on Connectedness to Humanity and to the Natural World." *Psychological Reports* 120, no. 1 (February 1): 102–17.

Baum, N. 2012. "Trap of Conflicting Needs: Helping Professionals in the Wake of a Shared Traumatic Reality." *Clinical Social Work Journal* 40, no. 1 (March): 37–45.

Beck, J. S. 2011. *Cognitive Behavior Therapy: Basics and Beyond* (2nd ed.). New York, NY: Guilford Press.

Berzoff, J., and E. Kita. 2010. "Compassion Fatigue and Countertransference: Two Different Concepts." *Clinical Social Work Journal* 38, no. 3 (September): 341–49.

Breslau, N. 2002. "Epidemiologic Studies of Trauma, Posttraumatic Stress Disorder, and Other Psychiatric Disorders." *Canadian Journal of Psychiatry* 47, no. 10 (December): 923–29.

Bride, B. E., M. Radey, and C. R. Figley. 2007. "Measuring Compassion Fatigue." *Clinical Social Work Journal* 35, no. 3 (June): 155–63.

Campagne, D. M. 2012. "When Therapists Run Out of Steam: Professional Boredom or Burnout?" *Revista de Psicopatologia y Psicologia Clinica* 17, no. 1: 75–85.

Cicognani, E., L. Pietrantoni, L. Palestini, and G. Prati. 2009. "Emergency Workers' Quality of Life: The Protective Role of Sense of Community, Efficacy Beliefs and Coping Strategies." *Social Indicators Research* 94, no. 3 (January): 449–63.

Clark, P. 2009. "Resiliency in the Practicing Marriage and Family Therapist." *Journal of Marital and Family Therapy* 35, no. 2 (April): 231–47.

Clear, J. 2018. *Atomic Habits: An Easy & Proven Way to Build Good Habits & Break Bad Ones*. New York: Random House.

Cloitre, M., K. C. Stovall-McClough, K. Nooner, P. Zorbas, et al. (2010). "Treatment for PTSD Related to Childhood Abuse: A Randomized Controlled Trial." *The American Journal of Psychiatry* 167, no. 8 (August): 915–24.

Duhigg, C. 2012. *The Power of Habit: Why We Do What We Do in Life and Business*. New York: Random House.

Friedman, M. J., P. A. Resick, R. Bryant, and C. R. Brewin. 2011. "Considering PTSD for DSM-5." *Depression and Anxiety* 28, no. 9 (September): 750–69.

Harr, C. 2013. "Promoting Workplace Health by Diminishing the Negative Impact of Compassion Fatigue and Increasing Compassion Satisfaction." *Social Work & Christianity* 40, no. 1: 71–88.

Hayes, S. C., K. D. Strosahl, and K. G. Wilson. 2012. *Acceptance and Commitment Therapy: The Process and Practice of Mindful Change* (2nd ed.). New York, NY: Guilford Press.

Kiecolt-Glaser, J. K., J. P. Gouin, and L. Hantsoo. 2010. "Close Relationships, Inflammation, and Health." *Neuroscience Biobehavioral Review* 35, no 1 (September): 33–38.

Koenen, K. C. and S. Galea. 2015. "Post-traumatic Stress Disorder and Chronic Disease: Open Questions and Future

Directions." *Social Psychiatry Psychiatric Epidemiology* 50 no. 4 (February): 511–13.

Larner, B., and A. Blow. 2011. "A Model of Meaning-Making Coping and Growth in Combat Veterans." *Review of General Psychology* 15, no. 3 (September): 187–97.

Lasiuk, G. C., and K. M. Hegadoren. 2006. "Posttraumatic Stress Disorder Part I: Historical Development of the Concept." *Perspectives in Psychiatric Care* 42, no. 1 (February): 13–20.

Linehan, M. M. 2015. *DBT Skills Training Manual* (2nd ed.). New York, NY: Guilford Press.

Linley, P. A., and S. Joseph. 2007. "Therapy Work and Therapists' Positive and Negative Well-Being." *Journal of Social and Clinical Psychology* 26, no. 3: 385–403.

Lloyd, C. and R. King. 2004. "A Survey of Burnout among Australian Mental Health Occupational Therapists and Social Workers." *Social Psychiatry Psychiatric Epidemiology* 39, no. 9 (September): 752–57.

Olff, M., W. Langeland, N. Draijer, and B. P. Gersons. 2007. "Gender Differences in Posttraumatic Stress Disorder." *Psychological Bulletin* 133, no. 2 (March): 183–204.

Pines, A., and C. Maslach. 1978. "Characteristics of Staff Burnout in Mental Health Settings." *Hospital Community Psychiatry* 29, no. 4 (April): 233–37.

Rae, G. 2010. "Alienation, Authenticity and the Self." *History of the Human Sciences* 23, no. 4 (August): 21–36.

Roberts, A. L., S. E. Gilman, J. Breslau, N. Breslau, and K. C. Koenen. 2011. "Race/Ethnic Differences in Exposure to Traumatic Events, Development of Post-traumatic Stress Disorder, and Treatment-Seeking for Post-traumatic Stress Disorder in the United States." *Psychological Medicine* 41, no. 1 (January): 71–83.

Rosenberg, T. and M. Pace. 2006. "Burnout among Mental Health Professionals: Special Considerations for the Marriage and Family Therapist." *Journal of Marital and Family Therapy* 32, no. 1 (January): 87–99.

Rytwinski, N. K., M. D. Scur, N. C. Feeny, and E. A. Youngstrum. 2013. "The Co-occurrence of Major Depressive Disorder among Individuals with Posttraumatic Stress Disorder: A Meta-analysis." *Journal of Traumatic Stress* 26, no. 3 (June): 299–309.

Scott, K. M., K. C. Koenen, S. Aquilar-Gaxiola, J. Alonso, et al. 2013. "Associations between Lifetime Traumatic Events and Subsequent Chronic Physical Conditions: A Cross-National, Cross-Sectional Study." *PLoS ONE* 8, no. 11 (November): e80573. https://doi.org/10.1371/journal.pone.0080573.

Slocum-Gori, S., D. Hemsworth, W. Chan, A. Carson, and A. Kazanjian. 2013. "Understanding Compassion Satisfaction, Compassion Fatigue and Burnout: A Survey of the Hospice Palliative Care Workforce." *Palliative Medicine* 27, no. 2 (February): 172–78.

Sprang, G., C. Craig, and J. Clark. 2011. "Secondary Traumatic Stress and Burnout in Child Welfare Workers: A Comparative Analysis of Occupational Distress across Professional Groups." *Child Welfare* 90, no. 6 (January): 149–68.

Tedeschi, R. G., J. Shakespeare-Finch, K. Taku, and L. G, Calhoun. 2018. *Posttraumatic Growth: Theory, Research, and Applications.* New York: Routledge.

Thompson, I. A., E. S. Amatea, and E. S. Thompson. 2014. "Personal and Contextual Predictors of Mental Health

Counselors' Compassion Fatigue and Burnout." *Journal of Mental Health Counseling* 36, no. 1 (January): 58–77.

Titchener, E. B. 1916. *A Text-Book of Psychology*. New York, NY: MacMillan.

Tyson, J. 2007. "Compassion Fatigue in the Treatment of Combat-Related Trauma during Wartime." *Clinical Social Work Journal* 35, no. 3 (July): 183–92.

Umberson, D. and J. Montez. 2010. "Social Relationships and Health: A Flashpoint for Health Policy." *Journal of Health and Social Behavior* 51, no. 1 (October): S54–S66.

Van Der Kolk, B. 2014. *The Body Keeps the Score: Brain, Mind, and Body in the Healing of Trauma*. New York, NY: Penguin Books.

Walker, M. 2017. *Why We Sleep: Unlocking the Power of Sleep and Dreams*. New York, NY: Scribner Press.

INDEX

ACKNOWLEDGMENTS

Every long journey has signposts along the way to help you get where you are going. The people in my life have provided me with the necessary reminders that I am moving forward and gaining ground.

From professors early in my professional journey, I gained tolerance for ambiguity and an awareness of the need to never get too attached to a hypothesis. From Susan Love, my first clinical supervisor, I gained the ability to laugh at myself and appreciate the humanity of every patient I treat. From the psychiatrists at the first psychiatric hospital I worked at, I gained appreciation for a succinct conceptualization of a case. From my many clinical colleagues throughout the years, I gained awareness of the need to take care of myself and never stop caring. From my current peer supervision group, I gained the connection and support I needed for my day-to-day work.

I recognize my children, Christopher, Bruce, Dominic, Cherie, Raymond, and Patrick, for every part of myself that I like best. Being your mother made me want to be a better person, even though I fall short like every mom. Being the children of a clinical therapist is not always easy, but you all seem to take it in stride. Unlike my pursuit of my master's or PhD degrees, at least you didn't have to suffer as I wrote this book.

I am grateful to my good friends throughout the years for their anchoring support and amazing cheerleading abilities. Much of what I know about my deepest darkness and personal overcoming has come from long talks with friends like Jodi Ussher and Thom Baltisberger and my brother Mark Gilbert. Without you, I wouldn't be me.

Finally, I must thank my love, Daryl, for your support while I wrote this book. You heard all the doubts and frustrations and urged me on. You happily picked up takeout so I could write some more. As I always say, I am the luckiest woman in the universe because we found each other.

Finally, I must acknowledge the privilege of working with the courageous patients I have treated over the 25 years of my career. For one therapy hour at a time, you share your struggles and I witness your resilience. It is because of you I have faith in humanity.

ABOUT THE AUTHOR

Trudy Gilbert-Eliot, PhD, LMFT, is a licensed psychotherapist in Las Vegas, Nevada. She received her master of science from California State University, Chico, and her PhD from Capella University in Minnesota. She specializes in working with first responders and is a contractor with the Las Vegas Metropolitan Police Department. She has worked with trauma survivors throughout her 25-year career, including abused children, survivors of domestic violence, psychiatric patients, addicts, and alcoholics, and most recently with military personnel, veterans, and first responders. She has also provided psychological support for those impacted by critical incidents, including mass shootings, hostage situations, suicides, and armed robberies. Currently in private practice, she supervises other marriage and family therapists and alcohol and drug counselors and teaches workshops for the University of Nevada, Reno.

9 781641 527569